THE
CAST-IRON
BAKING
BOOK

THE
CAST-IRON
BAKING
BOOK

More Than 175 Delicious Recipes for Your Cast-Iron Collection

Dominique DeVito

CIDER MILL PRESS

BOOK PUBLISHERS

Kennebunkport, Maine

Dedication:
Thank you, Barbara Bagner Goldstein, for your encouragement,
advice, and recipe suggestions. You are an inspiration and an angel.

13-Digit ISBN: 9781604336528
10-Digit ISBN: 1604336528

This book may be ordered by mail from the publisher. Please include $5.95 for postage and handling.
Please support your local bookseller first!

Books published by Cider Mill Press Book Publishers are available at special discounts for bulk purchases in the
United States by corporations, institutions, and other organizations. For more information, please contact the publisher.

Cider Mill Press Book Publishers
"Where Good Books Are Ready for Press"
12 Spring Street
PO Box 454
Kennebunkport, Maine 04046

Visit us on the Web! www.cidermillpress.com

Cover design by Alicia Freile, Tango Media
Interior design by Alicia Freile, Tango Media
Typography: Avenir, Fairfield, Fenway Park, Gotham, Journal, Linotype Centennial,
Minion, Neo Retro Draw, and Influence Medium

All images are used under official license from Shutterstock.com

Printed in China

1 2 3 4 5 6 7 8 9 0
First Edition

CONTENTS

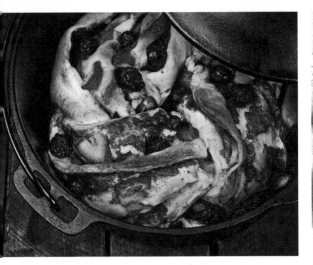

THE HISTORY OF CAST-IRON COOKWARE

WHY CAST IRON IS HERE TO STAY

There's nothing particularly attractive about a cast-iron skillet on the outside. It's all black, no shiny chrome, no flashy stainless steel, and it's heavy. And the handles get hot. And if the pan hasn't been properly cared for, it can get rusty or look grungy, which is how many of them end up at flea markets, where the dust really shows on them because they're…black.

But boy-oh-boy is there something attractive about a cast-iron skillet that's in good shape and properly cared for. In sum, it is one of the best cooking tools you can have.

AND HERE'S WHY:

Cast iron gets hot and distributes and holds heat like no other pan, which gives you a greater range of temperatures to work with. For example, if you're sautéing onions in a stainless-steel skillet, it gets hot quickly, and it also loses its heat exponentially when it is removed from it or the heat is lowered. Sautéed onions are best when cooked slowly and evenly so they caramelize without burning. When your cast-iron skillet is good and hot and you've started the process, you can lower the heat and know that the temperature won't fall off so much that you have to play with it as you continue to cook. And that's just one example.

Cast-iron skillets can go directly from the stove to the oven, and from the oven to the table, saving a lot of additional dishes for serving and a lot of time at clean-up. Yes, the handles get hot, but they're an extension of the skillets themselves and so will never melt or fall off.

Another great thing about the cast iron is the material itself—iron. Women, especially, tend to be diagnosed with iron deficiencies in their modern-day diets. Beneficial iron leaches into foods cooked in the cast-iron skillet. It won't compensate for iron deficiency, but it's helpful—and certainly better than the chemicals leaching from "nonstick"

coatings, which have been shown to contribute to liver damage, developmental problems, cancer, and early menopause.

If you aren't sold yet, there's the durability of cast iron. These skillets are family heirlooms; they last as long as they're maintained properly. In fact, there's something wonderful about a cast-iron skillet that's been passed down from mother to daughter, father to son, grandparent to grandchild. There are stories in your family's cast-iron skillets, and there are stories you'll be telling about yours.

THE HISTORY OF CAST-IRON COOKWARE

Cast iron is the product of pouring molten iron into a mold, letting it cool, and then refining it for its purpose (whether it be a pot, a bench, a piece of equipment, etc.). The Chinese were the first to develop foundries that could manage this, and it's estimated to date back several hundred years BC. Here in the West, iron foundries are estimated to date back to the 11th century. Large cauldrons were some of the first cooking implements to come out of the foundries, and they were prized for being able to hold a lot, maintain temperatures, and sit solidly over a fire. Just as in ancient China, the process of making cast-iron pieces in the West involved pouring the hot metal into a mold made from sand and, when cast, removing the sand mold and grinding the piece to smooth its surfaces.

Fast-forward to our European ancestors in the mid-19th century, where cooking was done in hearths. The cookware was adapted so that pieces could be moved or repositioned more easily, and cast-iron cauldrons were built with longer handles and legs. Dutch ovens—compact cookware closely resembling what we call Dutch ovens today—were forged to be placed directly on coals. As the oven itself evolved, the flat cast-iron skillet was created for use on an open "burner" or to be placed in the closed part of the cook stove.

AN AMERICAN EVOLUTION

Here in America, the first cast-iron foundry was established in 1619. Early settlers to the United States brought cookware with them, of course, and fashioned their hearths in the styles of what they were used to in their homelands. Cooking continued to be done in fireplaces or over open fires until modern plumbing made it possible to access water from faucets in the home. Cooks rejoiced, and running water became part of a true kitchen. Wood and coal fueled the fires that enabled cooking and heating of homes until gas companies developed ways to make ovens fueled by gas in the 1900s. It didn't take too much longer for electric ovens to come onto the scene—in the 1930s—though they didn't become really popular until the price of electricity fell, in

the 1960s. Through all these developments, cast iron remained the cookware of choice because it was still the most durable and practical.

It wasn't until after World War II—in the late 1940s/early 1950s—that stainless steel and aluminum emerged as materials for pots and pans. The factories that had been making guns and tanks had a lot of it, and the fact that these metals were lighter in weight than cast iron and didn't rust made them highly desirable by homemakers. In quick succession all manner of pots and pans were formed with these metals, and a nonstick coating was developed to make their care even easier. Teflon was approved by the US Food and Drug Administration in 1960, and its popularity took off, pushing cast iron to the back of the cabinet.

THE RESURGENCE OF ITS USE AND POPULARITY

It seems cooks started dragging the cast-iron skillets out from the backs of their pantries in earnest again by the late 2000s. The trend was confirmed when the *LA Times* published an article in November 2012 declaring, "Cast iron enjoys a comeback among cooks." The author, Noelle Carter, attributed part of the resurgence to the fact that the company making the cookware—Lodge Manufacturing— had introduced pre-seasoned cast iron. According to Lodge, this was an industry first that has now become an industry standard, as it eliminates having to continually reseason the cookware.

For me, personally, I have skillets and Dutch ovens that I've inherited, and some that I've purchased. Being careful to care for the cookware (as detailed in the next chapter), I have found it to always live up to my expectations. My cast-iron cookware heats beautifully and without smoking even without the addition of oil or fat in the skillet; the things I cook in it come out without sticking to the surface; it's a joy to be able to start something on the stove and then finish it in the oven; they seem to get better and better with use (which is not true of

Teflon-coated pans); and maybe best of all, my kids have taken to using them and discovering their simplicity and practicality (though I have to remind them about not using soap to clean them).

When the assignment came to write a book focused on baking in cast iron, I was worried that I couldn't come up with enough recipes. Turns out, as usual, that a cook is really only limited by his or her time and imagination. When I realized I could make any number of variations to boxed cake mixes, my family almost got sick of the variations I came up with. After the initial worry about heating up the lid of the Dutch oven in the bread-making process (I was concerned about melting in the high heat, which didn't happen), I learned that there is nothing yummier than a loaf cooked in a cast-iron Dutch oven. The crust is always great, and the inside airy and light.

WHICH PIECES FOR WHICH DISHES?

Now that cast iron is popular again, you can find skillets and other pieces in a range of sizes. If you do an online search for cast-iron cookware, you'll find two names that come up a lot: Lodge and Williams-Sonoma. Lodge is a manufacturer (see more about Lodge on the following pages), and you can buy pieces directly from them, or from retailers that sell their products. A manufacturer of enamel-coated cast iron is the French company Le Creuset. Williams-Sonoma sells it in many colors and sizes, and it's beautiful (if heavy). As with most things, you'll get what you pay for with your cast iron, too. A simple skillet may look pricey compared to stainless steel or Teflon, but considering you'll be using it almost daily for decades and it'll just be getting better, it's a necessary investment. Lodge and Le Creuset are manufacturers you can completely trust.

Lodge makes skillets ranging from 3.5 inches in diameter up to 13.25 inches in diameter. They also make deep skillets, griddles (and covers), Dutch ovens, and specialized bakeware like cornstick pans and mini cake pans. You are welcome to experiment with any of the sizes, but here's great news: For all the recipes in this book, I used just three sizes: a skillet ranging from 10 to 12 inches, a 4.5-quart Dutch oven, and a 7.5-quart Dutch oven.

Seasoning Versus Pre-Seasoned

The concept of seasoning a cast-iron skillet or other piece of cookware is to protect it from rusting and to aid in proper cooking. Part of the reason cast iron fell out of favor with home cooks was that keeping the cookware properly seasoned was an essential chore. When Lodge introduced pre-seasoned cast iron in the early 2000s, keeping the cookware seasoned became a whole lot easier. The cookware now has a nice sheen and surface that ensures great results right from the start. The seasoning process Lodge does to its cookware uses vegetable oil, just as cooks were instructed to do when seasoning their unseasoned cookware for the first time. And it doesn't hurt a pre-seasoned piece to get "re-seasoned" using the process outlined in the next section.

The important thing is the maintenance of the cookware. When it is washed (without soap), dried thoroughly (including the bottom, sides, and handles), and rubbed with enough vegetable oil to give it a smooth shine without appearing oily, then the cookware is ready for its next assignment.

Lodge Manufacturing

The history of the oldest U.S. manufacturer of cast-iron cookware is impressive. It all started when Joseph Lodge settled with his family in South Pittsburg, Tennessee in the late 1800s. Lodge opened the Blacklock Foundry there in 1896, named after a minister who was a friend. A fire struck in 1910, and the foundry was rebuilt just blocks from its original location. It was renamed the Lodge Manufacturing Company. Next came two World Wars and the Great Depression. The factory managed to survive by casting decorative pieces for a richer clientele until it could get back to focusing on cookware. The family persisted in modernizing its facility. Two neighboring foundries closed by the 1940s. Business wasn't booming for Lodge after that, either, but it survived because of the quality and durability of the product and the efficiency with which its products were—and continue to be—made. The breakthrough for the company was the introduction of pre-seasoned pieces, which took the confusion out of prepping the cookware for use. Another reason cast iron made a comeback is because the seasoning is non-toxic (vegetable oil)—which became important when Teflon's role in health problems started to be questioned. And of course, the cookware will have a very long lifetime.

Today, the factory is thriving in the otherwise sleepy town of South Pittsburg, Tennessee, whose population hovers at about 3,300. Nearly everyone knows someone who works for Lodge. A 2014 report in Bloomberg Business said, "According to the Cookware Manufacturers Association, shipments of cast iron and similar enameled products in the U.S. have increased more than 225 percent since 2003—rising from $35 million to more than $114 million—while shipments of cookware in general increased by just a third." That's good news for Lodge, which celebrates its 120th anniversary in 2016. The challenge now becomes how to maintain the popularity of something, that, with proper care, you don't really need to buy another of for about 100 years. Last but not least, if you're ever in South Pittsburg, you can visit the Lodge Factory Store, where over 2,000 products are sold, and if you go in late April, you might catch the National Cornbread Festival (www.nationalcornbread.com). Thank you, Lodge!

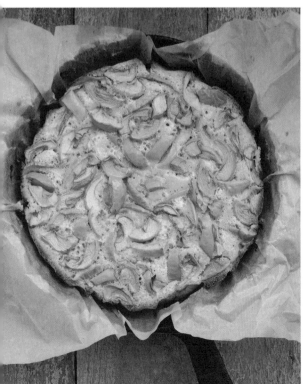

THE CARE & KEEPING OF YOUR CAST-IRON COOKWARE

We cooks have so many options when it comes to preparing foods: ovens, stoves, microwaves, grills, stainless steel, crockery, electric slow cookers, and woks. Among all these choices, a very old cooking tool—cast iron— is experiencing a renaissance of sorts in the modern kitchen. When you season and prep cast iron and start using it to make the delectable selection of recipes in this cookbook, you'll soon discover why it has stood the test of time—and is redefining the modern family's practices.

You may already be familiar with a cast-iron skillet. It's the plain, black, one-piece pan that always seemed to be at the back of the stack of fry pans in the cupboard. If you can remember where you saw that old pan, by all means, go get it. Acquiring a piece of cast-iron cookware from someone in your family is a way of keeping history alive. You'll be carrying on a tradition of cooking and serving foods that has been passed through generations. If, on the other hand, you're new to using cast iron and you are the one to acquire it in your family, you can look forward to sharing its results with your family and to someday passing it on to your children or grandchildren.

Besides being an amazing piece of cookware, cast iron does, indeed, last a lifetime (or more)—so long as it's properly cared for. It's simple enough to do, but it's important to do it properly, not only before you use a pan for the first time but before and after every use. Here's how it is done.

SEASONING A NEW SKILLET

When I went shopping for a new cast-iron skillet, I came upon Lodge pans—a company that has been making cast-iron skillets since the late 1800s. They brand themselves as "America's Original Cookware." Since nothing stands completely still, they have recently developed a method to season their cookware so that it will last as it always has but with minimal (consistent) care. That's a good thing! What they do is coat the pan with vegetable oil and bake it in at very high heat, which is just what you need to do to an unseasoned pan. With a new Lodge seasoned piece, you can be cooking from it almost immediately.

But let's start at the beginning, with an unseasoned skillet. Here's the procedure to bring it into use:

1. Wash with hot, soapy water.

2. Rinse and dry thoroughly.

3. If there's any rust on the pan, sand it lightly with fine-grained sandpaper. Apply Coca-Cola to the rust spots and leave on for 10 to 15 minutes. Wash again with soapy water, rinse, dry and put the skillet on a burner over low heat to dry any excess moisture.

4. If there's no rust, after drying the cookware all over, apply a light layer of cooking oil (vegetable oil, NOT olive oil, butter, or margarine!) all over the pan with a paper towel, rubbing even the handle. The pan should have a light sheen to it.

5. Place the skillet upside down on the middle rack of the oven and preheat the oven to 400 degrees (with the pan inside). Put a piece of foil or a baking dish on the lower rack to catch any drips of oil. Let the pan cook in the oven for about 2 hours.

6. Turn the oven off and let the pan cool (upside down) in the oven.

7. Take it out, wipe it down with a clean paper towel, and it's good to go.

8. If your pan has taken on a slightly brown color, you can repeat the process, which will further season the pan and darken its color, improving its appearance. This will also happen over time.

CARING FOR YOUR CAST IRON

Rule #1: Never wash your seasoned pan with soapy water!

Rule #2: Never put a cast-iron pan in the dishwasher!

Why? Soap breaks down the protective seasoning, and you have to re-season the pan all over again. Leaving any kind of water on the pan will lead to rusting, which will demand re-seasoning from the beginning. It seems counter-intuitive, especially when you're used to thinking "it's not clean unless it's been washed in (really) hot, soapy water," but it's actually a great thing about cast iron.

After you've cooked in your skillet, clean it with hot water (no soap) and a plastic, rough-surfaced scrub brush. Dry the cookware completely (all over) after washing. Put a teaspoon of vegetable oil in the pan and, with a paper towel, rub it in all over the pan until it has a nice sheen. Take a fresh paper towel and wipe the cookware dry. Store it where there is good air circulation so no moisture is trapped on it. If you need to stack it, put paper towels on the top and bottom.

GIVE IT A LOT OF LOVE

The best thing to do with your cast-iron skillet is USE IT! When you start using it for all the different things it can do (as evidenced by the diversity of recipes in this book), you'll probably find that the skillet lives on your stovetop, waiting for its next assignment. The more you use it, the better it gets. Nothing will stick to its surface. You can go from the frying pan to the fire, as it were, starting a dish on the stove and finishing it in the oven. You can cook your skillet to a very high heat (or put it in the campfire), and it'll cook up the food you put in it beautifully (so long as you keep an eye on it).

In short, with regular use, the cast-iron skillet truly is a pan that will just keep cooking and cooking, getting better and better with age and use. Just like you and me!

BREAKFAST TREATS & PASTRIES

A fresh-brewed cup of coffee calls for a breakfast treat or pastry. It's actually not that time-consuming to put something together—and cutting into fresh-baked coffee cake or breaking apart a still-warm, fruity scone is a simple pleasure that can ripple through your day. So go for it! Here is a collection of recipes that are guaranteed to brighten the mornings for you, your family, friends, roommates, co-workers, your dog(s)—everyone! Using a cast-iron skillet to cook breakfast also connects you to a feeling of tradition. You can imagine pioneers and homesteaders reaching for their skillets while wondering what was next for them as they headed West. You can imagine a farmer's wife cracking just-gathered eggs into a hot skillet in anticipation of her husband and children finishing the first round of milking and chores on the dairy farm. In our kitchens and lives, surrounded by the latest technology, there's nothing like breakfast prepared in a cast-iron skillet. So get baking!

STICKY BUNS

SERVES 6 ✦ ACTIVE TIME: 90 MINUTES ✦ START TO FINISH: 2 HOURS

This takes a bit of preparation time, but the result is sooo worth it! Your family or friends will wake up to the smell of these baking, and you'll soon have a kitchen full of people happily waiting for these to come out of the oven.

1 (26.4-oz.) package frozen biscuits

All-purpose flour for dusting

½ cup chopped pecans, toasted

1 teaspoon ground cinnamon

¼ teaspoon nutmeg

4 tablespoons butter, softened

¾ cup firmly packed light brown sugar

1 cup confectioner's sugar

3 tablespoons half-and-half

½ teaspoon vanilla extract

1. Preheat the oven to 375 degrees.

2. Lightly dust a flat surface with flour. Spread the frozen biscuit dough out in rows of 4 biscuits each. Cover with a dish cloth and let sit for about 30 minutes until the dough is thawed but still cool.

3. While dough is thawing, toast the pecans. Spread the pieces on a cookie sheet and bake for about 5 minutes, stirring the pieces with a spatula about halfway through. Be sure not to overcook. Allow to cool. Put the pieces in a bowl and add the cinnamon and nutmeg, stirring to coat the nuts with the spices.

4. Sprinkle flour over the top of the biscuit dough, and fold the dough in half, then press it out to form a large rectangle (approximately 10 inches by 12 inches). Spread the softened butter over the dough.

5. Sprinkle the brown sugar over the butter, then the seasoned nuts. Roll the dough with the butter, sugar, and nuts in it, starting with a long side. Cut into 1-inch slices and place in a lightly greased skillet.

6. Bake at 375 degrees for about 30-35 minutes, until rolls in the center are cooked through. Remove from the oven and allow to cool.

7. Make the glaze by mixing the confectioner's sugar, half-and-half, and vanilla. Drizzle over the warm rolls and serve.

Variations

✴ Substitute toasted walnut or almond pieces instead of the pecans for a nuttier, earthier flavor.

✴ Substitute dark brown sugar instead of the light brown sugar if you want more of a molasses flavor.

✴ Save a few calories (not many!) by using low-fat milk instead of half-and-half, or skip the glaze entirely and either serve without it, or drizzle some maple syrup over the rolls.

BLUEBERRY SCONES

SERVES 4 TO 6 ✦ ACTIVE TIME: 30 MINUTES ✦ START TO FINISH: 50 MINUTES

These are delicious whenever you eat them, but they're especially good about 15 minutes after you take them out of the oven, slathered with butter!

3 cups flour

⅓ cup sugar

2½ teaspoons baking powder

½ teaspoon baking soda

1 teaspoon salt

¾ cup (1½ sticks) unsalted butter, chilled and cut into pieces

1 tablespoon orange zest

1 cup milk or half-and-half

1 cup fresh blueberries

1. Preheat the oven to 400 degrees. Position a rack in the middle of the oven.

2. In a large bowl, whisk together the flour, sugar, baking powder, baking soda, and salt. Add the butter pieces and mix with an electric mixer until just blended, or mix with a fork so that the dough is somewhat crumbly.

3. Stir in the orange zest and milk, and gently fold in the blueberries, being careful not to overmix.

4. With flour on your hands, transfer the dough to a lightly floured surface. Form the dough into a circle about ½-inch thick. With a long knife, cut the dough into 12 wedges.

5. Butter the skillet, and put the scone wedges in a circle in it, leaving some space between the pieces. Bake for 20 to 25 minutes, or until golden.

6. If desired, sprinkle with some additional sugar when just out of the oven.

Variations

✺ Substitute fresh cranberries for the blueberries, or use a blend of ½ cup blueberries and ½ cup cranberries.

✺ Substitute dried fruit for the blueberries: ½ cup dried cherries or dried sweetened cranberries.

Blueberries split when cooked and their juices can get a little messy. If you want a neater-looking scone, you can use dried blueberries. Reduce the amount used by about half, though, as their flavor is also more concentrated.

SAVORY SCONES

SERVES 4 TO 6 ✦ ACTIVE TIME: 30 MINUTES ✦ START TO FINISH: 50 MINUTES

These cheesy scones with extra black pepper are a nice complement to scrambled eggs. You can also split them and use them as the bread for a nice ham-and-egg breakfast sandwich. Or enjoy them in the afternoon with a cup of tea.

2 cups flour

1 teaspoon baking powder

½ teaspoon salt

1 teaspoon freshly ground black pepper

½ teaspoon dry mustard

4 tablespoons butter, chilled, cut into pieces

½ cup grated sharp cheddar cheese

½ cup milk

1 egg beaten with a little milk

1. Preheat the oven to 400 degrees. Position a rack in the middle of the oven.

2. In a large bowl, whisk together the flour, baking powder, salt, pepper, and dry mustard. Add the butter pieces and mix with an electric mixer until just blended, or mix with a fork so that the dough is somewhat crumbly.

3. Stir in the cheese and milk, being careful not to overmix.

4. With flour on your hands, transfer the dough to a lightly floured surface. Form the dough into a circle about ½-inch thick. With a long knife, cut the dough into 6 to 8 wedges.

5. Butter the skillet, and put the scone wedges in a circle in it, leaving some space between the pieces.

6. Brush with the beaten egg. Bake for 20 to 25 minutes, or until golden.

Variation

Substitute ½ cup freshly grated aged cheese like Pecorino-Romano or a nutty-flavored cheese like Havarti for some different flavor profiles.

For an added breakfast treat, include bacon bits in the dough. Add about 1/3 cup crumbled bacon or bacon bits to the dough when adding the cheese and milk.

CHEDDAR JALAPEÑO SCONES

SERVES 4 TO 6 ✦ ACTIVE TIME: 30 MINUTES ✦ START TO FINISH: 50 MINUTES

The spiciness of the jalapeño livens up any breakfast. I like to split the cooked scones in half and top with a spoonful of sour cream and some sliced avocado.

2 cups flour

1 teaspoon baking powder

½ teaspoon salt

1 teaspoon freshly ground black pepper

4 tablespoons butter, chilled, cut into pieces

¾ cup grated sharp cheddar cheese

½ cup sliced or chopped jalapeño peppers

½ cup milk

1 egg beaten with a little milk

1. Preheat the oven to 400 degrees. Position a rack in the middle of the oven.

2. In a large bowl, whisk together the flour, baking powder, salt, and pepper. Add the butter pieces and mix with an electric mixer until just blended, or mix with a fork so that the dough is somewhat crumbly.

3. Stir in the cheese, peppers, and milk, being careful not to overmix.

4. With flour on your hands, transfer the dough to a lightly floured surface. Form the dough into a circle about ½-inch thick. With a long knife, cut the dough into 6 to 8 wedges.

5. Butter the skillet, and put the scone wedges in a circle in it, leaving some space between the pieces.

6. Brush with the beaten egg. Bake for 20 to 25 minutes, or until golden.

Variation

Ramp up the heat by substituting Pepper Jack cheese for the cheddar, or substitute a serrano pepper for the jalapeño.

Wear gloves when working with hot peppers so you don't get the oils in your eyes or other thin-skinned areas, as they irritate and burn.

SOUR CREAM AND DILL SCONES

SERVES 4 TO 6 ✦ ACTIVE TIME: 30 MINUTES ✦ START TO FINISH: 50 MINUTES

Dill is so fragrant and distinctive—you either like it or you don't. If you do, these scones will have you coming back for seconds or thirds. Try serving them with smoked salmon.

2 cups flour

1 teaspoon baking powder

½ teaspoon salt

1 teaspoon freshly ground black pepper

4 tablespoons butter, chilled, cut into pieces

¾ cup sour cream

1 tablespoon finely chopped fresh dill

1 egg beaten with a little milk

1. Preheat the oven to 400 degrees. Position a rack in the middle of the oven.

2. In a large bowl, whisk together the flour, baking powder, salt, and pepper. Add the butter pieces and mix with an electric mixer until just blended, or mix with a fork so that the dough is somewhat crumbly.

3. Stir in the sour cream and dill, being careful not to overmix.

4. With flour on your hands, transfer the dough to a lightly floured surface. Form the dough into a circle about ½-inch thick. With a long knife, cut the dough into 6 to 8 wedges.

5. Butter the skillet, and put the scone wedges in a circle in it, leaving some space between the pieces.

6. Brush with the beaten egg. Bake for 20 to 25 minutes, or until golden.

ROSEMARY BLACK PEPPER SCONES

SERVES 4 TO 6 ✦ ACTIVE TIME: 30 MINUTES ✦ START TO FINISH: 50 MINUTES

While these are a bit savory for an early breakfast, they are a hit for brunch, when they can very nicely complement a simple omelet and a mimosa with fresh orange juice.

3 cups flour

2½ teaspoons baking powder

½ teaspoon baking soda

1 teaspoon salt

¾ cup (1½ sticks) unsalted butter, chilled and cut into pieces

1 tablespoon crumbled dried rosemary

1 tablespoon freshly ground black pepper

1 cup milk or half-and-half

1. Preheat the oven to 400 degrees. Position a rack in the middle of the oven.

2. In a large bowl, whisk together the flour, baking powder, baking soda, and salt. Add the butter pieces and mix with an electric mixer until just blended, or mix with a fork so that the dough is somewhat crumbly.

3. Stir in the rosemary, black pepper, and milk, being careful not to overmix.

4. With flour on your hands, transfer the dough to a lightly floured surface. Form the dough into a circle about ½-inch thick. With a long knife, cut the dough into 12 wedges.

5. Butter the skillet, and put the scone wedges in a circle in it, leaving some space between the pieces. Bake for 20 to 25 minutes, or until golden.

OLIVE-FETA SCONES

SERVES 4 TO 6 ✦ ACTIVE TIME: 30 MINUTES ✦ START TO FINISH: 50 MINUTES

Here's a recipe that shines with the flavors of Greece and the Mediterranean. Another great accompaniment to eggs at breakfast, or salad at lunch, or eggplant parmigiana at dinner. Who's hungry?

1¾ cups all-purpose flour

2 teaspoons baking powder

¼ teaspoon salt

6 tablespoons unsalted butter, chilled, cut into pieces

½ cup crumbled feta cheese

½ cup pitted Kalamata olives, chopped, drained on paper towels

1 teaspoon ground black pepper

½ cup plain yogurt

5 tablespoons milk, divided

1. Preheat the oven to 400 degrees.

2. In a large bowl, whisk together the flour, baking powder, and salt. Add 4 tablespoons of the butter pieces and mix with an electric mixer until just blended, or mix with a fork so that the dough is somewhat crumbly. Stir in the feta, olives, and pepper.

3. In small bowl, combine yogurt with 3 tablespoons of the milk. Add this to the flour mixture and stir until the dough comes together. It will be moist.

4. With flour on your hands, transfer the dough to a lightly floured surface. Form the dough into a circle about ½-inch thick. With a long knife, cut the dough into 6 to 8 wedges.

5. Melt the additional 2 tablespoons butter in the skillet, and put the scone wedges in a circle in it, leaving some space between the pieces. Brush with the remaining milk, and bake for 20 to 25 minutes, or until golden.

FRENCH TOAST

SERVES 3 TO 6 ✦ ACTIVE TIME: 20 MINUTES ✦ START TO FINISH: 40 MINUTES

French toast—a great way to use up bread that's on the verge of going stale—is so simple and so satisfying.

6 eggs

1 cup milk

½ teaspoon vanilla extract

Pinch of nutmeg, if desired

6 slices, thick-cut bread

4 to 6 tablespoons butter

1. In a mixing bowl, combine the eggs, milk, vanilla, and nutmeg (if desired).

2. Place the slices of bread in a baking dish. Pour the egg mixture over the bread, shaking the pan to distribute evenly. Flip the pieces of bread a couple of times to coat both sides with the mixture.

3. Heat 2 tablespoons butter in the skillet over medium-high heat. Add 2 slices of bread to the pan and cook until golden brown on each side, 2 to 3 minutes a side. Transfer the cooked pieces to a warm plate or keep warm in the oven while you cook the additional pieces.

4. Serve with maple syrup or jam.

Variation

If you want to make gluten-free French toast, just use gluten-free bread. It's as simple and delicious as that. You'll want one that's got some thickness to it and minimal crust.

The secret to great French toast is the choice of bread and the amount of egg mixture that saturates the bread. If you use a basic sandwich bread, you won't need as much egg mixture. If you use an egg-based bread like Challah, or a sourdough bread, you'll need more egg mixture as these kinds of bread are denser. They will also need to sit in the egg mixture longer. You'll need to adjust the recipe for the type of bread you're using, so be sure to have some extra eggs and milk on hand.

MAPLE FRENCH TOAST

SERVES 4 ✦ ACTIVE TIME: 20 MINUTES ✦ START TO FINISH: 40 MINUTES

What better to do with leftover crusty bread than to soak it in some fresh eggs and cream, sizzle it up in some butter, and drizzle it with maple syrup? Enjoy it with strong coffee and thick-sliced bacon, that's what.

4 eggs

½ cup heavy cream

¾ cup all-natural maple syrup

8 slices slightly stale, thick-cut bread

4 tablespoons butter

1. Preheat the oven to 200 degrees and place an oven-proof serving dish in it.

2. In a small bowl, combine the eggs, heavy cream, and ½ cup of the maple syrup. Whisk to thoroughly combine, or use an immersion blender.

3. Put pieces of bread in a 13x19-inch baking dish and cover with the egg mixture. Let the bread soak up the egg mixture for about 20 minutes, turning halfway so both sides can soak.

4. Heat a 12-inch skillet over medium heat. Add 2 tablespoons of the butter and as it melts, tilt the pan to coat it evenly. When the butter is heated but not browned, add 4 slices of the soaked bread. Allow to cook for about 4 minutes, then flip them. Drizzle the pieces with maple syrup while they're cooking on the other side, and after another 4 minutes or so, flip them again so the side with the maple syrup gets cooked for a minute or so.

5. Transfer the cooked pieces to the serving dish in the oven. Repeat the cooking process for the remaining slices of bread. Before serving, warm the maple syrup (add some additional syrup) in a microwave-safe container for 30 seconds. Test the warmth. You don't want to over-warm it, just take the chill out. Serve the French toast with maple syrup.

Many kinds of bread can be used to make French toast, from simple sandwich bread to hearty whole-grain loaves. The thicker the bread, the longer you should let it soak (up to overnight if desired). I like using country breads from a bakery that I can slice at home, especially when adding some maple syrup to the eggs and cream, which adds some sweetness. The sugar in the maple syrup will also caramelize on the skillet, which is great as long as the heat is kept on medium, so it won't burn the sugar but simply "toast" it.

CINNAMON BUNS

SERVES 6 ✦ ACTIVE TIME: 60 MINUTES ✦ START TO FINISH: 90 MINUTES

There's something about serving these fresh out of the skillet that makes them even more special than they already are. If you love the smell (and taste) of cinnamon, you will gobble these up.

1 (26.4-oz.) package frozen biscuits

All-purpose flour for dusting

2 teaspoons ground cinnamon

¾ cup firmly packed dark brown sugar

4 tablespoons butter, softened

1 cup confectioner's sugar

3 tablespoons half-and-half

½ teaspoon vanilla extract

1. Preheat the oven to 375 degrees.

2. Lightly dust a flat surface with flour. Spread the frozen biscuit dough out in rows of 4 biscuits each. Cover with a dish cloth and let sit for about 30 minutes until the dough is thawed but still cool.

3. Mix the cinnamon and brown sugar in a small bowl.

4. When the dough is ready, sprinkle flour over the top and fold it in half, then press it out to form a large rectangle (approximately 10x12 inches). Spread the softened butter over the dough, then the cinnamon/sugar mix. Roll up the dough, starting with a long side. Cut into 1-inch slices and place in a lightly greased skillet.

5. Bake at 375 degrees for about 35 minutes, until rolls are cooked through in the center. Remove from the oven and allow to cool slightly.

6. Make the glaze by mixing the confectioner's sugar, half-and-half, and vanilla. Drizzle over the warm rolls and serve.

Cinnamon is a spice with a long history of health benefits as well as culinary delights. The cinnamon sticks sold in stores are actually "quills" from cinnamon trees; they're the inner bark. Cinnamon is grown in India, Sri Lanka, Indonesia, Madagascar, Brazil, and parts of the Caribbean. Its smell is said to invigorate cognitive functions and its compounds have antibacterial and analgesic properties. It is used in sweet and savory dishes.

SKILLET APPLE PANCAKE

SERVES 4 TO 6 ✦ **ACTIVE TIME: 30 MINUTES** ✦ **START TO FINISH: 60 MINUTES**

Make this the morning after you go apple picking. It's a great way to use up some of the apples and get your day off to a great start.

4 eggs

1 cup milk

3 tablespoons sugar

½ teaspoon vanilla extract

½ teaspoon salt

¾ cup flour

4 tablespoons butter

2 apples, peeled, cored and thinly sliced

¼ teaspoon cinnamon

Dash of ground nutmeg

Dash of ground ginger

¼ cup light brown sugar

Confectioner's sugar for sprinkling (optional)

1. Preheat the oven to 425 degrees.

2. In a large bowl, whisk together the eggs, milk, sugar, vanilla, and salt. Add the flour and whisk to combine. Set the batter aside.

3. Heat the skillet over medium-high heat and add the butter, tilting the pan to thoroughly coat the bottom. Add the apple slices and top with the cinnamon, nutmeg, and ginger. Stir, cooking until apples begin to soften, about 5 minutes. Add the brown sugar and continue to stir while cooking for an additional few minutes until apples are very soft. Pat the cooked apples along the bottom of the skillet to distribute evenly.

4. Pour the batter over the apples, coating them evenly. Transfer the skillet to the oven and bake for about 20 minutes until it is browned and puffed. Sprinkle with confectioner's sugar when fresh out of the oven if desired. Serve immediately.

Variation

To make a gluten-free version of this recipe, just substitute the ¾ cup of flour with ¾ cup Gluten Free All-Purpose Baking Flour from Bob's Red Mill and add 1 teaspoon of xanthan gum. Mix together before whisking into your wet ingredients.

You can vary the fruit-spice combo for this recipe in multiple ways. Consider making it with pears instead of apples, or using 1 of each. Add raisins to the apples or pears while cooking (about 1/2 cup), or try cranberries, blueberries, or dried cherries, along with toasted walnuts (about 1/2 cup).

SKILLET BERRY PANCAKE

SERVES 4 TO 6 ✦ ACTIVE TIME: 30 MINUTES ✦ START TO FINISH: 60 MINUTES

Just as making this with fresh apples is a way to celebrate after picking them, so is throwing together fresh summer berries to make this is a true treat when strawberries, blueberries, raspberries, and blackberries are in season. (If they're not, you can use thawed frozen fruits and pretend it's summer.)

4 eggs

1 cup milk

3 tablespoons sugar

½ teaspoon vanilla extract

½ teaspoon salt

¾ cup flour

4 tablespoons butter

½ cup sliced strawberries

½ cup blueberries

¼ cup honey

1. Preheat the oven to 425 degrees.

2. In a large bowl, whisk together the eggs, milk, sugar, vanilla, and salt. Add the flour and whisk to combine. Set the batter aside.

3. Heat the skillet over medium-high heat and add the butter, tilting the pan to thoroughly coat the bottom. Add the berries and honey. Stir, cooking, until just softened and the honey coats the fruit, about 5 minutes. Shake the skillet gently to distribute the fruit evenly over the bottom.

4. Pour the batter into the skillet. Transfer the skillet to the oven and bake for about 20 minutes until it is browned and puffed. Serve immediately.

DAVID EYRE'S PANCAKE

SERVES 4 ◆ **ACTIVE TIME: 30 MINUTES** ◆ **START TO FINISH: 30 MINUTES**

A friend shared this recipe that she found in The New York Times *years ago. Turns out it has quite the following. It's more like a popover than a pancake, but it's really delicious. David Eyre was a writer/editor, so I'm happy to include this tribute to him and hopefully create a whole new following for it.*

½ cup flour

½ cup milk

2 eggs, lightly beaten

Pinch of nutmeg

4 tablespoons butter

2 tablespoons confectioner's sugar

Juice of half a lemon

1. Preheat the oven to 425 degrees.

2. In a bowl, combine the flour, milk, eggs, and nutmeg. Beat lightly; leave the batter a little lumpy.

3. Melt the butter in the skillet and, when very hot, pour in the batter.

4. Transfer the skillet to the oven and bake for 15 to 20 minutes, until golden brown.

5. Sprinkle with the sugar, return briefly to the oven, then remove. Sprinkle with lemon juice and serve.

This "pancake" is usually served with jam, which leads to all kinds of flavor options. Try anything from a sweet strawberry jam to a more pungent orange marmalade or fig spread. In the fall, an apple or pear butter would be perfect.

CORN CAKES

SERVES 4 ✦ ACTIVE TIME: 30 MINUTES ✦ START TO FINISH: 60 MINUTES

These breakfast treats are grittier and mealier than fluffy wheat-flour pancakes. But with pats of butter melted on top, they are even tastier!

1 cup yellow cornmeal

½ cup whole wheat flour

3 tablespoons sugar

1 tablespoon baking powder

¼ teaspoon salt

2 large eggs

1¼ cups milk

½ teaspoon vanilla extract

3 tablespoons butter, plus more as needed

1. Preheat the oven to 200 degrees.

2. In a large bowl, whisk together the cornmeal, flour, sugar, baking powder, and salt. In a small bowl, combine eggs, milk, and vanilla. Pour the egg mixture into the dry ingredients and stir to combine. It's ok if the batter is a bit lumpy.

3. Heat the skillet over medium-high heat and melt some butter in it. When hot, make pancakes by spooning the batter into the pan. Cook for about 2 minutes on each side, until golden. Keep the pancakes warm on a plate in the oven. Serve with lots of butter.

Variation

Make gluten-free corn cakes by substituting ½ cup gluten-free all-purpose baking flour for the whole wheat flour. Add ½ teaspoon xanthan gum, as well.

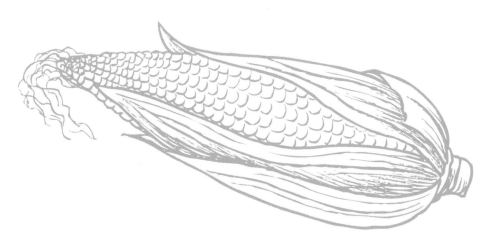

If you have leftover corn on the cob, cut the kernels off of one, break them apart, and add them to the batter before cooking. They'll add texture, flavor, and some moisture. Consider serving with a sweet-spicy salsa, like one that has peaches in it.

CINNAMON COFFEE CAKE

SERVES 6 TO 8 ✦ ACTIVE TIME: 90 MINUTES ✦ START TO FINISH: 2 HOURS

Some people sprinkle cinnamon over their coffee before brewing it. Cinnamon is not only wonderfully fragrant, but also a natural antioxidant and anti-inflammatory and helps to fight infection.

Cake

1¾ cup flour

⅔ cup sugar

½ teaspoon baking soda

¼ teaspoon salt

¼ teaspoon ground cinnamon

8 tablespoons (1 stick) butter, softened

2 eggs

1 teaspoon vanilla extract

¾ cup buttermilk

Topping

1 cup flour

½ cup sugar

½ cup dark brown sugar

½ teaspoon cinnamon

¼ teaspoon salt

6 tablespoons unsalted butter, softened

1. Preheat the oven to 325 degrees.

2. To make the cake, whisk together the flour, sugar, baking soda, salt, and cinnamon in a large bowl. Add the butter and stir with an electric mixer until blended.

3. In a small bowl, whisk together the eggs, vanilla, and buttermilk. Pour into the flour mixture and blend on high speed until the batter is light and fluffy. Pour the batter into a greased skillet.

4. To make the topping, whisk together the flour, sugars, cinnamon, and salt in a bowl. Add the softened butter and combine to form a crumbly dough.

5. Dot the topping over the cake in the skillet. Put the skillet in the oven and bake for 45 minutes, until knife inserted in the middle comes out clean. Allow to cool for about 10 minutes before serving.

ALMOND COFFEE CAKE

SERVES 6 TO 8 ✦ ACTIVE TIME: 90 MINUTES ✦ START TO FINISH: 2 HOURS

Toasted almonds and almond extract impart a heavenly taste and fragrance to this traditional morning cake.

Cake

1¾ cup flour

⅔ cup sugar

½ teaspoon baking soda

¼ teaspoon salt

8 tablespoons (1 stick) butter, softened

2 eggs

1 teaspoon almond extract

½ cup buttermilk

Topping

½ cup sugar

½ cup dark brown sugar

½ teaspoon ginger

¼ teaspoon salt

¾ cup (1½ sticks) unsalted butter, melted

2 cups flour

½ cup dried organic coconut

1. Preheat the oven to 325 degrees.

2. To make the cake, whisk together the flour, sugar, baking soda, and salt in a large bowl. Add the butter and stir with an electric mixer until blended.

3. In a small bowl, whisk together the eggs, almond extract, and buttermilk. Pour in the flour mixture and blend on high speed until the batter is light and fluffy. Pour the batter into a greased skillet.

4. To make the topping, whisk together the sugars, ginger, and salt in a bowl. Add the melted butter and combine. Then add the flour and coconut and stir to form a crumbly dough.

5. Dot the topping over the cake in the skillet. Put the skillet in the oven and bake for 45 minutes, until knife inserted in the middle comes out clean. Allow to cool for about 10 minutes before serving.

Variation

A delicious gluten-free variation can be made by substituting 1 cup almond flour and ¾ gluten-free all-purpose baking flour (any blend or brand will do) for the 1¾ cup flour in the cake, and add 1 teaspoon xanthan gum. For the topping, substitute 1 cup gluten-free all-purpose baking flour and 1 cup gluten-free rolled oats (be sure the oats were processed in a gluten-free facility; choose Bob's Red Mill brand if there's any question). If the topping seems too dry, add up to 2 additional tablespoons of butter, one at a time.

Fresh fruit is a great addition to this coffee cake. Before putting on the topping, sprinkle in some peeled, chopped pears, or some blueberries, or pears and cranberries.

BLUEBERRY COFFEE CAKE

SERVES 6 TO 8 ✦ ACTIVE TIME: 90 MINUTES ✦ START TO FINISH: 2 HOURS

One of the things I love about summer is how early it gets light in the morning. It's easy to get up at 5:30 or 6:00 a.m. when the sun is out, and that's the perfect time to make this coffee cake with summer-fresh, ripe blueberries. Of course, it's not so bad in the dead of winter, either, with blueberries you froze from the summertime. They don't even need to be thawed first.

Cake

1¾ cup flour

⅔ cup sugar

½ teaspoon baking soda

¼ teaspoon salt

8 tablespoons (1 stick) butter, softened

2 eggs

1 teaspoon vanilla extract

½ cup buttermilk

2 cups blueberries

Topping

1 cup flour

½ cup sugar

½ cup dark brown sugar

½ teaspoon ginger

¼ teaspoon salt

6 tablespoons unsalted butter, softened

½ cup crushed walnut pieces (optional)

1. Preheat the oven to 325 degrees.

2. To make the cake, whisk together the flour, sugar, baking soda, and salt in a large bowl. Add 6 tablespoons of butter and stir with an electric mixer until blended.

3. In a small bowl, whisk together the eggs, vanilla, and buttermilk. Pour into the flour mixture and blend on high speed until the batter is light and fluffy.

4. Over medium heat, melt the additional 2 tablespoons butter in the skillet. Add the blueberries and shake to distribute evenly. Cook the blueberries in the butter for a couple of minutes, then pour the batter over them.

5. To make the topping, whisk together the flour, sugars, ginger, and salt in a bowl. Add the softened butter and combine to form a crumbly dough. Stir in the walnut pieces.

6. Dot the topping over the cake in the skillet. Put the skillet in the oven and bake for 45 minutes, until knife inserted in the middle comes out clean. Allow to cool for about 10 minutes before serving.

APPLESAUCE OATMEAL BREAD

SERVES 6 TO 8 ✦ ACTIVE TIME: 30 MINUTES ✦ START TO FINISH: 90 MINUTES

This is an easy bread to make for a delicious after-school snack. It's practically cake, but with far less sugar. Adding flax seeds bumps up the nutritional goodness without compromising the flavor or texture of the bread.

¾ cup sugar

2 large eggs

½ cup vegetable oil

1 teaspoon vanilla extract

½ cup whole wheat flour

1 cup all-purpose flour

¼ teaspoon baking powder

½ teaspoon baking soda

1 teaspoon cinnamon

¼ teaspoon nutmeg

½ teaspoon salt

½ cup rolled oats

¾ cup chunky applesauce

¼ cup flax seeds (optional)

½ cup chopped walnuts or slivered almonds (optional)

1. Preheat the oven to 350 degrees. Put the skillet in the oven while it preheats.

2. In a large bowl, mix together the sugar, eggs, oil, and vanilla. In a separate bowl, combine the flours, baking powder, baking soda, cinnamon, nutmeg, and salt. Add the dry ingredients to the bowl of wet ingredients. Stir until thoroughly combined. Next, add the oats, applesauce, flax seeds, and nuts. Stir to combine.

3. Using pot holders or oven mitts, carefully remove the skillet from the oven. Pour the batter in and dust the top with additional oats and some brown sugar if desired. Bake for 45 minutes until the bread sounds hollow when tapped on the top and a toothpick or knife inserted in the middle comes out clean.

4. Let rest for about 5 to 10 minutes. Gently invert onto a plate. Allow to cool before cutting into wedges and serving.

PUMPKIN BANANA BREAD

MAKES 1 LOAF ✦ ACTIVE TIME: 30 MINUTES ✦ START TO FINISH: 2 HOURS

Whenever you can find something to add pumpkin to, go for it. Pumpkin is such a great source of Vitamin A, carotenoids, fiber, and more. It adds a ton of moisture to breads like this. The combination of pumpkin and banana is really yummy. If you like walnuts, be sure to add them, too. This is delicious as a bread to go with coffee, as a healthy breakfast on the go, or as a not-too-sweet dessert with a dollop of Greek yogurt on top of a slice.

8 tablespoons (1 stick) butter, softened

⅔ cup light brown sugar

2 tablespoons honey

2 large eggs

1 cup pumpkin purée (unsweetened)

1 cup mashed very ripe bananas (about 2 or 3)

2 tablespoons water

1 teaspoon vanilla extract

1½ cups flour (white or whole wheat)

¼ teaspoon baking powder

1 teaspoon baking soda

¾ teaspoon salt

½ teaspoon ground cinnamon

½ teaspoon ground nutmeg

½ cup chopped walnuts (optional)

1. Preheat the oven to 350 degrees. Put the skillet in the oven while it preheats.

2. In a large bowl, beat together the butter, sugar, honey, eggs, pumpkin, banana, water, and vanilla. In a separate bowl, whisk together the flour, baking powder, baking soda, salt, cinnamon, and nutmeg. Add the dry ingredients to the bowl of wet ingredients. Stir until thoroughly combined. Fold in the chopped walnuts.

3. Using pot holders or oven mitts, carefully remove the skillet from the oven. Pour in the batter and return the skillet to the oven. Bake for about 60 minutes, until the bread sounds hollow when tapped on the top and a toothpick or knife inserted in the middle comes out clean.

4. Let rest for about 20 minutes. Gently invert onto a plate. Allow to cool before cutting into wedges and serving.

PALEO PUMPKIN BANANA BREAD

This is an easy recipe to convert to one that's Paleo, though we're leaving the skillet behind.

3 bananas, mashed

4 eggs

1 cup pumpkin purée (unsweetened)

¼ cup honey

⅓ cup coconut oil, melted

⅓ cup coconut flour

3 tablespoons arrowroot starch

1 teaspoon cinnamon

½ teaspoon baking soda

¼ teaspoon salt

1. Preheat the oven to 350 degrees.

2. Combine all the ingredients, stirring well. Grease a loaf pan with coconut oil before pouring the batter in.

3. Bake for about 50 minutes, until the bread sounds hollow when tapped on the top and a toothpick or knife inserted in the middle comes out clean.

4. Allow to cool before cutting into slices.

Variation

Increase the moisture and flavor of this bread by adding ½ cup flaked, unsweetened coconut.

BREADS THAT RISE TO THE OCCASION

Wait until you taste the mouth-watering breads that will be coming out of your oven when you start baking with a cast-iron skillet and cast-iron Dutch Oven! You'll find that things are cooked more evenly, and that as a result of the alchemy that happens with baking (which is what ultimately yields something that tastes amazing rather than simply good), yields the best-tasting breads, buns, flatbreads, and more. Because grain-based breads have been cooked over fires since our earliest days, I incorporated recipes for breads made around the world, like naan from India, soda bread from Ireland, focaccia from Italy, and even Ethiopian injera. There are also lots of recipes for family favorites that can be made quickly and easily, such as pizzas, calzones, and focaccias

BASIC WHITE BREAD

MAKES 1 SMALL ROUND ✦ ACTIVE TIME: 25 MINUTES ✦ START TO FINISH: 3 HOURS

I was skeptical of the recipes I found for baking bread in a cast-iron Dutch oven. They called for heating the cookware in the oven while the oven preheated (to a very high 450 degrees) and leaving the lid on for part of the baking time. But the photos looked good, so I dove in. This was the first recipe I made, and it was a great success and huge hit. I'm definitely a convert. Hope you will be, too.

¼ teaspoon active dry yeast

¼ teaspoon sugar

1½ cups water (110 to 115 degrees)

1 teaspoon kosher salt

3 cups all-purpose flour plus more for kneading and dusting

1. Put the yeast and sugar in a measuring cup and add about ½ cup warm water in a drizzle. Hot water will kill the yeast, so it's important that the water be warm without being hot. Cover the measuring cup with plastic wrap and set it aside for about 15 minutes. If the yeast doesn't foam, it is not alive and you'll need to start over.

2. When the yeast is proofed, pour it into a large bowl and add the additional cup of warm water. Stir gently to combine. Add the salt to the flour, and add the flour to the yeast mixture. Stir with a wooden spoon until combined. The dough will be wet and sticky.

3. Put a dusting of flour on a flat surface and lift out the dough. With flour on your hands and more at the ready, begin kneading the dough so that it loses its stickiness. Don't overdo it, and don't use too much flour; just enough that it is more cohesive.

4. Place the dough in a large bowl, cover the bowl with plastic wrap, and allow to rise untouched for at least one hour, and up to several hours. Gently punch it down, recover with the plastic, and allow to rise again for another 30 minutes or so.

5. While the dough is on its final rise, preheat the oven to 450 degrees. Put a piece of parchment paper on the bottom of the Dutch oven and put it in with the lid on so it gets hot. When the oven is ready and dough has risen, carefully remove the lid and gently scoop the dough from the bowl into the pot. Cover and bake for 15 minutes. Remove the lid and continue to bake for another 15 to 20 minutes until the top is golden and it sounds hollow when tapped.

6. Remove the pot from the oven and use tea towels to carefully remove the bread. Allow to cool before slicing.

It's important to "proof" the yeast before adding it to your recipe to ensure that it is fresh and active. If it is, it reacts with the sugar and liquid and creates tiny bubbles. It also releases a smell that is described (appropriately enough) as "yeasty"—the smell you get from fresh-baked bread. Yeast reacts with sugar to release carbon dioxide and, eventually, alcohol. This is the basis of making beer and wine, too. But with baking, the fermentation process stops when the live cells are cooked in the oven.

WHEAT BREAD

SERVES 4 TO 6 ✦ ACTIVE TIME: 20 MINUTES ✦ START TO FINISH: 60 MINUTES

When you discover how easy it is to make such a tasty loaf of bread with all-purpose flour, you'll want to start experimenting with other flavors and textures, found in flours, nuts, and so on. Here's a wheat bread recipe that uses enough all-purpose flour to ensure adequate rising and fluffiness upon baking.

¼ teaspoon instant yeast

¼ teaspoon sugar

1½ cups water (110 to 115 degrees)

1 teaspoon kosher salt

2 cups whole wheat flour

1 cup all-purpose flour plus more for kneading and dusting

1. Put the yeast and sugar in a measuring cup and add about ½ cup warm water in a drizzle. Hot water will kill the yeast, so it's important that the water be warm without being hot. Cover the measuring cup with plastic wrap and set it aside for about 15 minutes. If the yeast doesn't foam, it is not alive and you'll need to start over.

2. When the yeast is proofed, pour it into a large bowl and add the additional cup of warm water. Stir gently to combine. Add the salt to the flour, and add the flour to the yeast mixture. Stir with a wooden spoon until combined. The dough will be wet and sticky.

3. Put a dusting of flour on a flat surface and lift out the dough. With flour on your hands and more at the ready, begin kneading the dough so that it loses its stickiness. Don't overdo it, and don't use too much flour; just enough that it is more cohesive.

4. Place the dough in a large bowl, cover the bowl with plastic wrap, and allow to rise untouched for at least one hour, and up to several hours. Gently punch it down, recover with the plastic, and allow to rise again for another 30 minutes or so.

5. While the dough is on its final rise, preheat the oven to 450 degrees. Put a piece of parchment paper on the bottom of the Dutch oven and put it in with the lid on so it gets hot. When the oven is ready and dough has risen, carefully remove the lid and gently scoop the dough from the bowl into the pot. Cover and bake for 15 minutes. Remove the lid and continue to bake for another 15 to 20 minutes until the top is golden and it sounds hollow when tapped.

6. Remove the pot from the oven and use tea towels to carefully remove the bread. Allow to cool before slicing.

Variations

● Making this with a seeded crust really boosts the flavor and adds texture, too. A nice combination is toasted sesame seeds with poppy seeds. When the dough is in the Dutch oven and ready to be baked, sprinkle generously with the seeds, pressing just lightly to help the seeds adhere.

● Gluten-Free Variation: Make a gluten-free whole grain loaf by mixing one 20-ounce bag of Bob's Red Mill Hearty Whole Grain Bread mix with 1¾ cup water, 2 eggs, ¼ cup vegetable oil, and 2 teaspoons cider vinegar. There's an envelope of yeast in the package. Allow it to proof in the water, mix in the other ingredients, knead, and allow to rise about 45 minutes before baking in the Dutch oven as you would for the Wheat Bread recipe.

WHOLE WHEAT CRANBERRY-PECAN BREAD

MAKES 1 SMALL ROUND ✦ ACTIVE TIME: 25 MINUTES ✦ START TO FINISH: 3 HOURS

This is a delicious and dense bread that is especially good toasted and served with fresh butter or cream cheese. It also makes a great complement to soft cheeses when cut into small pieces and served instead of crackers.

¼ teaspoon instant yeast

¼ teaspoon sugar

1½ cups water (110 to 115 degrees)

1 teaspoon kosher salt

2 cups whole wheat flour

1 cup all-purpose flour plus more for kneading and dusting

1 cup dried cranberries

1 cup chopped pecans

1. Put the yeast and sugar in a measuring cup and add about ½ cup warm water in a drizzle. Hot water will kill the yeast, so it's important that the water be warm without being hot. Cover the measuring cup with plastic wrap and set it aside for about 15 minutes. If the yeast doesn't foam, it is not alive and you'll need to start over.

2. When the yeast is proofed, pour it into a large bowl and add the additional cup of warm water. Stir gently to combine. Add the salt to the flour, and add the flour to the yeast mixture. Stir with a wooden spoon until combined. The dough will be wet and sticky.

3. Put a dusting of flour on a flat surface and lift out the dough. With flour on your hands and more at the ready, begin kneading the dough so that it loses its stickiness. As you're kneading, add in the cranberries and pecans so that they're distributed evenly in the dough. Don't overdo it, and don't use too much flour; just enough that it is more cohesive.

4. Place the dough in a large bowl, cover the bowl with plastic wrap, and allow to rise untouched for at least one hour, and up to several hours. Gently punch it down, recover with the plastic, and allow to rise again for another 30 minutes or so.

5. While the dough is on its final rise, preheat the oven to 450 degrees. Put a piece of parchment paper on the bottom of the Dutch oven and put it in with the lid on so it gets hot. When the oven is ready and dough has risen, carefully remove the lid and gently scoop the dough from the bowl into the pot. Cover and bake for 15 minutes. Remove the lid and continue to bake for another 15 to 20 minutes until the top is golden and it sounds hollow when tapped.

Variation

Substitute walnut pieces for the pecans, or do half walnuts and half pecans.

6. Remove the pot from the oven and use tea towels to carefully remove the bread. Allow to cool before slicing.

GLUTEN-FREE BREAD

MAKES 1 SMALL ROUND ✦ **ACTIVE TIME: 25 MINUTES** ✦ **START TO FINISH: 3 HOURS**

We are fortunate to live in a time when gluten-free options are numerous. If you love bread and can't or don't want to eat gluten, make this recipe and dig in! You'll be amazed at the result—an equally crusty yet fluffy loaf that tastes great!

½ teaspoon instant yeast

¼ teaspoon sugar

1½ to 2½ cups water
(110 to 115 degrees)

1 teaspoon kosher salt

1½ teaspoons xanthan
gum

3 cups Bob's Red Mill
gluten-free flour plus
more for kneading and
dusting

⅓ cup Bob's Red
Mill sweet rice flour
(glutinous rice flour)

1. Put the yeast and sugar in a measuring cup and add about ½ cup warm water in a drizzle. Hot water will kill the yeast, so it's important that the water be warm without being hot. Cover the measuring cup with plastic wrap and set it aside for about 15 minutes. If the yeast doesn't foam, it is not alive and you'll need to start over.

2. When the yeast is proofed, pour it into a large bowl and add an additional cup of warm water. Stir gently to combine. Add the salt and xanthan gum to the flour, and add the flour to the yeast mixture. Stir with a wooden spoon until combined. Add up to an additional cup of warm water to accommodate the rice flour, which is tackier than regular flour. The dough should be wet and sticky.

3. Put a dusting of flour on a flat surface and lift out the dough. With flour on your hands and more at the ready, begin kneading the dough so that it loses its stickiness. Don't overdo it, and don't use too much flour; just enough that it is more cohesive.

4. Place the dough in a large bowl, cover the bowl with plastic wrap, and allow to rise untouched for at least one hour, and up to several hours. Gently punch it down, recover with the plastic, and allow to rise again for another 30 minutes or so.

5. While the dough is on its final rise, preheat the oven to 450 degrees. Put a piece of parchment paper on the bottom of the Dutch oven and put it in with the lid on so it gets hot. When the oven is ready and dough has risen, carefully remove the lid and gently scoop the dough from the bowl into the pot. Cover and bake for 15 minutes. Remove the lid and continue to bake for another 15 to 20 minutes until the top is golden and it sounds hollow when tapped.

6. Remove the pot from the oven and use tea towels to carefully remove the bread. Allow to cool before slicing.

SEEDED BREAD

As you master bread making in the cast-iron Dutch oven, you can experiment in all kinds of ways. If you like toasted sesame seeds, this is a real treat.

¼ teaspoon instant yeast

¼ teaspoon sugar

1½ cups water (110 to 115 degrees)

1 teaspoon kosher salt

3 cups all-purpose flour plus more for kneading and dusting

1 egg yolk beaten with 1 tablespoon water

½ cup sesame seeds

1. Put the yeast and sugar in a measuring cup and add about ½ cup warm water in a drizzle. Hot water will kill the yeast, so it's important that the water be warm without being hot. Cover the measuring cup with plastic wrap and set it aside for about 15 minutes. If the yeast doesn't foam, it is not alive and you'll need to start over.

2. When the yeast is proofed, pour it into a large bowl and add the additional cup of warm water. Stir gently to combine. Add the salt to the flour, and add the flour to the yeast mixture. Stir with a wooden spoon until combined. The dough will be wet and sticky.

3. Put a dusting of flour on a flat surface and lift out the dough. With flour on your hands and more at the ready, begin kneading the dough so that it loses its stickiness. Don't overdo it, and don't use too much flour; just enough that it is more cohesive.

4. Place the dough in a large bowl, cover the bowl with plastic wrap, and allow to rise untouched for at least one hour, and up to several hours. On a gently floured surface, turn out the dough and gently punch it down. Put a large piece of parchment paper in the bowl in which the bread was rising before. Return the dough to the bowl on the parchment paper, cover with plastic wrap, and allow to rise again for another 30 minutes or so.

5. While the dough is on its final rise, preheat the oven to 450 degrees. Put a piece of parchment paper on the bottom of the Dutch oven and put it in with the lid on so it gets hot. When the oven is ready and dough has risen, carefully remove the lid and gently scoop the dough from the bowl into the pot, brush with the egg wash, and sprinkle generously with the sesame seeds. Cover and bake for 15 minutes. Remove the lid and continue to bake for another 15 to 20 minutes until the top is golden and it sounds hollow when tapped.

6. Remove the pot from the oven and use tea towels to carefully remove the bread. Allow to cool before slicing.

Variation

Substitute unsalted sunflower seeds or pepitas (pumpkin seeds) for the sesame seeds.

NO-KNEAD BREAD

MAKES 1 SMALL ROUND ✦ ACTIVE TIME: 20 MINUTES ✦ START TO FINISH: UP TO 2 DAYS

There is really nothing easier than this recipe for making a delicious loaf of fresh bread. The only thing is you need to give it up to two days, so plan ahead!

¼ teaspoon active
dry yeast

¼ teaspoon sugar

1½ cups water
(110 to 115 degrees)

1½ teaspoons kosher
salt

3 cups all-purpose
flour, plus more
for dusting

1. In a large bowl, add the yeast and sugar and top with the warm water. Stir to dissolve the yeast. Cover the bowl with plastic wrap and allow to proof for about 15 minutes. Add the flour and salt. Stir until just blended with the yeast and water. The dough will be sticky.

2. Cover the bowl with plastic wrap and set aside for at least 15 hours and up to 18 hours, preferably in a place that's 65 to 70 degrees.

3. The dough will be bubbled when you go to work with it. Lightly dust a work surface and scoop the dough out onto it. Dust your fingers with flour so they don't stick to the dough. Fold it gently once or twice.

4. Transfer the dough to a clean bowl that is room temperature and cover with a dish towel. Let rise another 1 to 2 hours until doubled in size.

5. While the dough is on its final rise, preheat the oven to 450 degrees, placing the Dutch oven inside with the lid on so it gets hot. When the oven is ready and dough has risen, carefully remove the lid and gently scoop the dough from the bowl into the pot. Cover and bake for 20 minutes. Remove the lid and continue to bake for another 25 minutes until the top is golden and it sounds hollow when tapped.

6. Remove pot from oven and use tea towels to carefully transfer bread to a rack or cutting board, and allow to cool at least 20 minutes before serving.

ROASTED GARLIC BREAD

MAKES 1 SMALL ROUND ✦ ACTIVE TIME: 25 MINUTES ✦ START TO FINISH: 3 HOURS

Be forewarned: If you love garlic (as I suspect you do if you want to make this recipe), the smell of this bread baking will make you drool. Once you can slice into it, eat it as-is, toast it and top with a thin smear of pesto, or serve it as a wonderful substitute for traditional garlic bread.

1 head garlic

¼ cup olive oil

¼ teaspoon instant yeast

¼ teaspoon sugar

1½ cups water (110 to 115 degrees)

1 teaspoon kosher salt

3 cups all-purpose flour plus more for kneading and dusting

1. Preheat the oven to 375 degrees.

2. Take as much of the paper skin off the head of garlic as possible without separating the cloves. With a sharp knife, cut off only as much of the top of the head as necessary to expose the cloves in their sleeves. Put the garlic cut side up on a piece of heavy duty aluminum foil or in a garlic roaster. Pour the olive oil over the top of the head of garlic. Fold the aluminum foil up and over the garlic to cover it, crimping any edges together, or put the lid on the garlic roaster. Roast in the oven for 50 to 60 minutes.

3. Open the foil or roaster and allow the garlic to cool slightly. Extract the roasted cloves from their sleeves by squeezing the bottom so the cloves pop out. Put them on a plate or in a shallow bowl. Keep the cooking oil.

4. Put the yeast and sugar in a measuring cup and add about ½ cup warm water in a drizzle. Hot water will kill the yeast, so it's important that the water be warm without being hot. Cover the measuring cup with plastic wrap and set it aside for about 15 minutes. If the yeast doesn't foam, it is not alive and you'll need to start over.

5. When the yeast is proofed, pour it into a large bowl and add the additional cup of warm water. Stir gently to combine. Add the salt to the flour, and add the flour to the yeast mixture. Stir with a wooden spoon until combined. The dough will be wet and sticky.

6. Put a dusting of flour on a flat surface and lift out the dough. With flour on your hands and more at the ready, begin kneading the dough so that it loses its stickiness. Don't overdo it, and don't use too much flour; just enough that it is more cohesive. Add the roasted garlic cloves while you're gently kneading the dough.

7. Lightly grease a large bowl with some of the garlic-infused olive oil and place the dough in it. Cover the bowl with plastic wrap, and allow to rise untouched for at least one hour, and up to several hours. Gently punch it down, recover with the plastic, and allow to rise again for another 30 minutes or so. Brush the surface with the garlic-infused oil.

8. While the dough is on its final rise, preheat the oven to 450 degrees. Put a piece of parchment paper on the bottom of the Dutch oven and put it in with the lid on so it gets hot. When the oven is ready and dough has risen, carefully remove the lid and gently scoop the dough from the bowl into the pot. Cover and bake for 15 minutes. Remove the lid and continue to bake for another 15 to 20 minutes until the top is golden and it sounds hollow when tapped.

9. Remove the pot from the oven and use tea towels to carefully remove the bread. Allow to cool before slicing.

Variation

Add ¼ cup fresh rosemary during the kneading process to complement the garlic and add another layer of flavor.

OLIVE LOAF

MAKES 1 SMALL ROUND ✦ **ACTIVE TIME: 25 MINUTES** ✦ **START TO FINISH: 3 HOURS**

I love the earthy-salty flavor of dark olives like Kalamatas. They are delicious in bread, too. Rather than taking the time to slice a lot of Kalamata olives, I like to use a top-shelf tapenade (olive) spread, which is easy to spread and distribute in the dough, too.

¼ teaspoon instant yeast

¼ teaspoon sugar

1½ cups water (110 to 115 degrees)

1 teaspoon kosher salt

3 cups all-purpose flour plus more for kneading and dusting

½ cup tapenade (olive spread) or ½ cup Kalamata olives

1 tablespoon olive oil

1. Put the yeast and sugar in a measuring cup and add about ½ cup warm water in a drizzle. Hot water will kill the yeast, so it's important that the water be warm without being hot. Cover the measuring cup with plastic wrap and set it aside for about 15 minutes. If the yeast doesn't foam, it is not alive and you'll need to start over.

2. When the yeast is proofed, pour it into a large bowl and add the additional cup of warm water. Stir gently to combine. Add the salt to the flour, and add the flour to the yeast mixture. Stir with a wooden spoon until combined. The dough will be wet and sticky.

3. Put a dusting of flour on a flat surface and lift out the dough. With flour on your hands and more at the ready, begin kneading the dough so that it loses its stickiness. Don't overdo it, and don't use too much flour; just enough that it is more cohesive. Incorporate the tapenade or olive pieces while you're kneading.

4. Place the dough in a large bowl, cover the bowl with plastic wrap, and allow to rise untouched for at least one hour, and up to several hours. Gently punch it down, recover with the plastic, and allow to rise again for another 30 minutes or so. Brush with the olive oil.

5. While the dough is on its final rise, preheat the oven to 450 degrees. Put a piece of parchment paper on the bottom of the Dutch oven and put it in with the lid on so it gets hot. When the oven is ready and dough has risen, carefully remove the lid and gently scoop the dough from the bowl into the pot. Cover and bake for 15 minutes. Remove the lid and continue to bake for another 15 to 20 minutes until the top is golden and it sounds hollow when tapped.

6. Remove the pot from the oven and use tea towels to carefully remove the bread. Allow to cool before slicing.

OLIVE OIL LOAF

MAKES 1 SMALL ROUND ✦ ACTIVE TIME: 25 MINUTES ✦ START TO FINISH: 3 HOURS

Make this bread when you are going tailgating or you have a crowd of people coming for lunch. When it's cooled, cut it in half like a cake, then make a giant sandwich with mayo, cold cuts, cheeses, tomatoes, onions, peppers—think of it as a round submarine sandwich loaf, but it'll taste so good! Serve in wedges with other picnic foods.

¼ teaspoon instant yeast

¼ teaspoon sugar

1½ cups water (110 to 115 degrees)

1 teaspoon kosher salt

3 cups all-purpose flour plus more for kneading and dusting

1 tablespoon freshly ground black pepper

1 tablespoon extra virgin olive oil

1. Put the yeast and sugar in a measuring cup and add about ½ cup warm water in a drizzle. Hot water will kill the yeast, so it's important that the water be warm without being hot. Cover the measuring cup with plastic wrap and set it aside for about 15 minutes. If the yeast doesn't foam, it is not alive and you'll need to start over.

2. When the yeast is proofed, pour it into a large bowl and add the additional cup of warm water. Stir gently to combine. Add the salt and pepper to the flour, and add the flour to the yeast mixture. Add the olive oil. Stir with a wooden spoon until combined. The dough will be sticky.

3. Put a dusting of flour on a flat surface and lift out the dough. With flour on your hands and more at the ready, begin kneading the dough so that it loses its stickiness. Don't overdo it, and don't use too much flour; just enough that it is more cohesive.

4. Place the dough in a large bowl, cover the bowl with plastic wrap, and allow to rise untouched for at least one hour, and up to several hours. On a piece of parchment paper, remove from the bowl and gently punch it down, shaping it into a round that will fit inside the Dutch oven (approximately 8 inches in diameter). Recover with the plastic and allow to rise again for another 30 minutes or so. Brush with the olive oil.

5. While the dough is on its final rise, preheat the oven to 450 degrees. Put a piece of parchment paper on the bottom of the Dutch oven and put it in with the lid on so it gets hot. When the oven is ready and dough has risen, carefully remove the lid and gently scoop the flattened dough from the bowl into the pot. Cover and bake for 15 minutes. Remove the lid and continue to bake for another 15 to 20 minutes until the top is golden and it sounds hollow when tapped.

6. Remove the pot from the oven and use tea towels to carefully remove the bread. Allow to cool completely.

HONEY BREAD

MAKES 1 SMALL ROUND ✦ ACTIVE TIME: 30 MINUTES ✦ START TO FINISH: 3 HOURS

The combination of honey and egg yolks in this bread creates something like a Challah—with a beautiful yellow color on the inside and toasty brown crust on the outside. The dense, buttery bread is slightly sweet, too. It's a lovely loaf for eating, toasting, and making French toast.

1 tablespoon active dry yeast

1 tablespoon sugar

3 tablespoons water

4 tablespoons butter

1 cup milk

¼ cup honey

1 tablespoon salt

2 egg yolks

3 cups flour

1 egg yolk beaten with 1 tablespoon milk

1. Put the yeast and sugar in bowl and add about ½ cup warm water in a drizzle. Hot water will kill the yeast, so it's important that the water be warm without being hot. Cover the bowl with plastic wrap and set it aside for about 15 minutes. If the yeast doesn't foam, it is not alive and you'll need to start over.

2. In a saucepan, melt the butter over low heat. Stir in the milk, honey, and salt. Remove from the heat and allow to cool slightly. Pour this over the yeast/sugar combination and stir.

3. Add the egg yolks and flour and stir with a wooden spoon until the flour is blended in well.

4. Put a dusting of flour on a flat surface and lift out the dough. With flour on your hands and more at the ready, begin kneading the dough so that it loses its stickiness. The kneading process will take about 10 minutes, forming an elastic, smooth dough.

5. Place the dough in a large bowl, cover the bowl with plastic wrap, and allow to rise in a warm spot, untouched for at least one hour, and up to several hours. Gently punch it down, recover with the plastic, and allow to rise again for another 30 minutes or so.

6. While the dough is on its final rise, preheat the oven to 450 degrees. Put a piece of parchment paper on the bottom of the Dutch oven and put it in with the lid on so it gets hot. When the oven is ready and dough has risen, carefully remove the lid and gently scoop the dough from the bowl into the pot. Cover and bake for 15 minutes. Remove the lid and brush the surface of the loaf with the egg/milk mixture. Continue to bake for another 15 to 20 minutes until the top is golden and it sounds hollow when tapped.

7. Remove the pot from the oven and use tea towels to carefully remove the bread. Allow to cool on a dish for 15 minutes or so before slicing.

CHOCOLATE-CINNAMON BREAD

**MAKES 1 SMALL ROUND ✦ DUTCH OVEN: 4.5 QUART ✦
ACTIVE TIME: 25 MINUTES ✦ START TO FINISH: 3 HOURS**

This is like an exotic pain au chocolat—*crunchy and crispy on the outside, fluffy yet chocolately and spicy on the inside. Be patient when it comes out of the oven and allow the bread to cool for 15 to 20 minutes so that it slices more easily and cleanly.*

¼ teaspoon active dry yeast

¼ teaspoon sugar

1½ cups lukewarm water

2 tablespoons unsalted butter

1 cup semi-sweet chocolate morsels

1 teaspoon ground cinnamon

3 cups all-purpose flour plus more for kneading and dusting

1 teaspoon salt

1. Put the yeast and sugar in a measuring cup and add about ½ cup lukewarm water in a drizzle. Hot water will kill the yeast, so it's important that the water be warm without being hot. Cover the measuring cup with plastic wrap and set it aside for about 15 minutes. If the yeast doesn't foam, it is not alive and you'll need to start over.

2. Cut the butter into thin slices and put it with the chocolate morsels in a medium-sized, microwave-safe bowl. Melt the chocolate and butter in the microwave, working in 20-second increments. After each 20 seconds, stir the butter and chocolate. Microwave just until melted, about 40 to 60 seconds. Stir in the cinnamon and set aside to cool. It must be cool when added to the dough.

3. When the yeast is proofed, pour it into a large bowl and add the additional cup of lukewarm water. Stir gently to combine. Add the salt to the flour, and add the flour to the yeast mixture. Stir with a wooden spoon until combined. The dough will be wet and sticky.

4. Put a dusting of flour on a flat surface and lift out the dough. With flour on your hands and more at the ready, begin kneading the dough so that it loses its stickiness. Don't overdo it, and don't use too much flour—just enough that it is more cohesive. While kneading, add the chocolate/cinnamon in increments, using as much as you want. You may not choose to use it all. Work it into the dough gently.

5. Place the dough in a large bowl, cover the bowl with plastic wrap, and allow to rise untouched for at least one hour, and up to several hours. Gently punch it down, recover with the plastic, and allow to rise again for another 30 minutes or so.

6. While the dough is on its final rise, preheat the oven to 450 degrees. Put a piece of parchment paper on the bottom of the Dutch oven and put it in with the lid on while the oven reaches 450 degrees. When the oven is ready, use pot holders to remove the lid of the Dutch oven, scoop the dough from the bowl to the pot, put the lid back on and close the oven door.

7. Bake with the lid on for 15 minutes, then remove the lid. Allow to bake for another 15 to 20 minutes until the top is golden and the bread sounds hollow when tapped.

8. Remove the pot from the oven and use tea towels to carefully remove the bread. Allow to cool before slicing.

Variation

Add a subtle yet delightful heat to the bread by adding 1 teaspoon cayenne pepper along with the cinnamon.

DINNER ROLLS

SERVES 8 TO 10 (ABOUT 12 ROLLS) ✦ ACTIVE TIME: 60 MINUTES ✦
START TO FINISH: 3 HOURS

These classic dinner rolls are light, flaky, and buttery perfection. Once found on the tables at fine restaurants everywhere, they're now commonly replaced by sliced loaf breads. See if these will even make it to your table when they come out of the oven.

1¼ cups whole milk, heated to 110 degrees

3 tablespoons sugar

1 tablespoon active dry yeast

8 tablespoons (1 stick) unsalted butter

¾ teaspoon salt

2 eggs at room temperature, lightly beaten

3½ cups cake or bread flour (not all-purpose flour)

1. In a small bowl, combine ½ cup warm milk and the sugar. Sprinkle the yeast over it, stir, and set aside so the yeast can proof (about 10 minutes).

2. While the yeast is proofing, melt the butter in the skillet over low to medium heat, and remove from heat when melted.

3. When the yeast mix is frothy, stir in 3 tablespoons of the melted butter, the remaining milk, the salt, and the eggs. Then stir in the flour, mixing until all ingredients are incorporated. Transfer to a lightly floured surface and knead the dough for 5 to 10 minutes until it is soft and springy and elastic.

4. Coat the bottom and sides of a large mixing bowl (ceramic is best) with butter. Place the ball of dough in the bowl, cover loosely with plastic wrap, put it in a naturally warm, draft-free location, and let it rise until doubled in size, about 45 minutes to 1 hour.

5. Prepare a lightly floured surface to work on. Punch down the dough in the bowl and transfer it to the floured surface. Warm the skillet with the butter so that it is melted again.

6. Break off pieces of the dough to form into rolls, shaping them into 2-inch balls with your hands. Roll the balls in the butter in the skillet, and leave them in the skillet as they're made and buttered.

7. Cover the skillet loosely with a clean dish towel, put it in the warm, draft-free spot, and let the rolls rise until doubled in size, about 30 minutes. While they're rising, preheat the oven to 350 degrees.

8. When the rolls have risen and the oven is ready, cover the skillet with aluminum foil and bake in the oven for 20 minutes. Remove the foil and finish cooking, another 15 minutes or so, until the rolls are golden on top and light and springy. Serve warm.

GARLIC ROSEMARY ROLLS

**SERVES 6 TO 8 (ABOUT 8 ROLLS) ✦ ACTIVE TIME: 90 MINUTES ✦
START TO FINISH: 3 HOURS**

If you're a fan of garlic as my family is, you will be swooned by the scent these rolls give off as they're baking. Better yet is the taste. Mangia!

1 packet active dry yeast (2¼ teaspoons)

1 cup water (110 to 115 degrees)

1 tablespoon sugar

1 tablespoon butter, melted

1 teaspoon salt

2 cloves garlic, minced

4 cups flour

1 teaspoon fresh rosemary leaves, chopped, or 2 teaspoons dried, crushed rosemary

1 tablespoon butter

1 egg, lightly beaten

Sea salt

1. In a large bowl, mix the yeast, warm water, and sugar and let the yeast proof for about 10 minutes, until foamy.

2. Next add the melted butter, salt, garlic, and half the flour. Mix until the dough forms a sticky dough. Continue to add flour, mixing to form a soft dough. Add the rosemary with the last addition of flour.

3. Coat the bottom and sides of a large mixing bowl (ceramic is best) with butter. Place the ball of dough in the bowl, cover loosely with plastic wrap, put it in a naturally warm, draft-free location, and let it rise until doubled in size, about 45 minutes to 1 hour.

4. Put the skillet in the oven and preheat the oven to 400 degrees.

5. Transfer the dough to a lightly floured surface. Divide into 8 pieces and form into balls.

6. Remove the skillet from the oven and melt the butter in it. Place the rolls in the skillet, turning to cover them with butter. Wash the rolls with the beaten egg and sprinkle with sea salt.

7. Bake in the oven until golden and set, about 40 minutes.

Make cheesy garlic-rosemary rolls by sprinkling Parmesan or pecorino romano cheese on the tops after washing with the beaten egg. Skip the sea salt.

SWEET POTATO ROLLS

**SERVES 8 TO 10 (MAKES 18 SMALL ROLLS) ✦ ACTIVE TIME: 60 MINUTES ✦
START TO FINISH: 3 HOURS**

There's something about the color and flavor of sweet potatoes that says "goodness." These rolls won't disappoint. They're delicious served with savory dishes like roast pork or chicken, but also great for breakfast with homemade jam.

1 large or 2 small sweet potatoes, peeled and cut into cubes

½ cup water (110 to 115 degrees)

1 packet active dry yeast (2¼ teaspoons)

2 tablespoons light brown sugar

2 cups all-purpose flour

¾ cup (1½ sticks) unsalted butter

⅓ cup honey

1 egg, lightly beaten

½ teaspoon salt

½ teaspoon ground ginger

¼ teaspoon ground nutmeg

1½ cups whole wheat flour

1. Cook the sweet potatoes by putting the cubes in a saucepan, covering them with water, bringing the water to a boil, and simmering them in the boiling water until they're soft, about 20 minutes. When they can be easily pierced with the tip of a knife, drain them in a colander. While they're warm, put them in a large bowl and mash them with a potato masher or fork.

2. In a large bowl, combine the yeast and the warm water. Add the brown sugar and ¼ cup of the flour, stirring well. Set aside so the yeast can proof (about 10 minutes).

3. Melt 5 tablespoons of the butter and add it to the large bowl with the sweet potatoes. Stir in the honey, egg, salt, ginger, and nutmeg. Stir well until smooth.

4. Add the sweet potato mixture to the yeast and stir to combine. Add the remaining all-purpose flour and the whole wheat flour. Stir to form a soft dough, adding additional whole wheat flour a tablespoon at a time until it holds together. Transfer to a lightly floured surface and knead the dough for 5 to 10 minutes until it is soft and springy and elastic.

5. Coat the bottom and sides of a large mixing bowl (ceramic is best) with 2 tablespoons of melted butter. Place the ball of dough in the bowl, cover loosely with plastic wrap, put it in a naturally warm, draft-free location, and let it rise until doubled in size, about 1 to 2 hours.

6. Prepare a lightly floured surface to work on. Punch down the dough in the bowl and transfer it to the floured surface. Warm the skillet with the butter so that it is melted again.

7. Break off 18 pieces of the dough to form into rolls, shaping them into balls with your hands. Roll the balls in the butter in the skillet, and leave them in the skillet as they're made and buttered.

8. Cover the skillet loosely with a clean dish towel, put it in the warm, draft-free spot, and let the rolls rise until doubled in size, about 30 minutes. While they're rising, preheat the oven to 375 degrees.

9. When the rolls have risen and the oven is ready, bake for 30 to 35 minutes until golden on the top. Serve warm.

BISCUITS

SERVES 4 TO 6 ✦ ACTIVE TIME: 20 MINUTES ✦ START TO FINISH: 40 MINUTES

For fluffy biscuits, you need to work with a very hot skillet. The golden brown crust on the bottom is as much of a delight as the airy, warm dough.

2 cups flour

1 teaspoon sugar

1 teaspoon salt

1 tablespoon baking powder

6 to 8 tablespoons butter, cut into pieces

½ cup + 2 tablespoons buttermilk

1. Preheat oven to 450 degrees.

2. In a large bowl, combine the flour, sugar, salt, and baking powder.

3. Using a fork or pastry knife, blend in 6 tablespoons of the butter to form crumbly dough. Form a well in the middle and add ½ cup buttermilk. Stir to combine and form a stiff dough. Using your fingers works best! If it seems too dry, add 1 tablespoon more of the buttermilk, going to 2 tablespoons if necessary.

4. Put 2 tablespoons butter in the skillet and put it in the oven to melt while the skillet heats.

5. Put the dough on a lightly floured surface and press out to a thickness of about 1 inch. Press out biscuits using an inverted water glass. Place the biscuits in the skillet and bake for about 10 minutes, until golden on the bottom.

Biscuits are another buttery bread that can be served with savory or sweet additions. You can make mini ham sandwiches by splitting the biscuits, putting some mayonnaise and grainy mustard on them, and putting in a slice of fresh-baked ham. You can fill them with scrambled eggs and bacon bits. Or you can slather them with butter and your favorite jam or honey. Or just eat them as-is.

GLUTEN-FREE BISCUITS

It is possible to make delicious gluten-free biscuits, though they'll be a bit more crumbly than those made with regular flour.

1½ cups rice flour

⅓ cup potato starch

3 tablespoons tapioca flour

1 tablespoon baking powder

3 teaspoons maple sugar, or 1 tablespoon maple syrup

2 teaspoons cream of tartar

¼ teaspoon salt

1 teaspoon xanthan gum

5 to 7 tablespoons butter

½ cup + 2 tablespoons buttermilk

1. Preheat oven to 450 degrees.

2. In a large bowl, combine the flours, baking powder, sugar, cream of tartar, salt, and xanthan gum. Using a fork or pastry knife, blend in 5 tablespoons of the butter to form crumbly dough.

3. Form a well in the middle and add ½ cup buttermilk. Stir to combine and form a stiff dough. Using your fingers works best! If it seems too dry, add 1 tablespoon more of the buttermilk, going to 2 tablespoons if necessary.

4. Put 2 tablespoons butter in the skillet and put it in the oven to melt while the skillet heats.

5. Put the dough on a lightly floured surface and press out to a thickness of about 1 inch. Press out biscuits using an inverted water glass. Place the biscuits in the skillet and bake for about 10 minutes, until golden on the bottom.

FOCACCIA

SERVES 4 TO 6 ✦ ACTIVE TIME: 90 MINUTES ✦ START TO FINISH: 3 HOURS

This is essentially a raised flatbread—like a crustier pizza—to which all kinds of yummy things can be added. It's become synonymous with Italian cuisine, and it's certainly popular in Italy, but it's also made throughout the Mediterranean countries, from Istria through southern France. You can find it in grocery stores, but there's nothing like a fresh piece right out of the skillet, still warm, with toppings just the way you want them. This one is a simple salt/Parmesan focaccia.

1 packet active dry yeast (2¼ teaspoons)

2 cups water (110 to 115 degrees)

4 to 4½ cups flour

2 teaspoons salt

3 tablespoons olive oil, plus more for drizzling over bread before baking

Sea salt (coarse grained) and freshly ground black pepper

Grated Parmesan for topping

1. Proof the yeast by mixing it with the warm water. Let sit for 10 minutes until foamy.

2. In a bowl, combine the flour, salt, and yeast mix. Stir to combine well. Transfer to a lightly floured surface and knead the dough until it loses its stickiness, adding more flour as needed, about 10 minutes.

3. Coat the bottom and sides of a large mixing bowl (ceramic is best) with olive oil. Place the ball of dough in the bowl, cover loosely with plastic wrap, put it in a naturally warm, draft-free location, and let it rise until doubled in size, about 45 minutes to 1 hour.

4. Preheat the oven to 450 degrees.

5. When risen, turn the dough out onto a lightly floured surface and divide it in half. Put a tablespoon of olive oil in the skillet, and press one of the pieces of dough into it. Drizzle some olive oil over it and sprinkle with salt and pepper, then with Parmesan cheese. Cover loosely with plastic wrap and let rise for about 20 minutes. With the other piece, press it out onto a piece of parchment paper and follow the same procedure to top it and let it rise.

6. Put in the middle of the oven and bake for 25 to 30 minutes until golden and hot. Remove from oven and let rest for 5 minutes before removing from skillet to cool further. Wipe any crumbs off the skillet, coat with some more olive oil, and transfer the other round to the skillet. Bake for about 25 minutes.

7. If desired, you can put the extra dough in a plastic bag and store it in the refrigerator for up to 3 days to use later.

ITALIAN HERB FOCACCIA

SERVES 4 TO 6 ◆ **ACTIVE TIME: 90 MINUTES** ◆ **START TO FINISH: 3 HOURS**

Infused with oregano, thyme, and basil—and with garlic, too—this herbed focaccia is sensational dipped into olive oil infused with red peppers, or topped with an olive tapenade.

1 teaspoon active dry yeast

1 cup water (110 to 115 degrees)

2 to 2½ cups flour

1 teaspoon salt

½ teaspoon dried oregano

½ teaspoon dried thyme

¼ teaspoon dried basil

1 clove garlic, minced

3 tablespoons olive oil, plus more for drizzling over bread before baking

Sea salt (coarse grained) and freshly ground black pepper

Grated Parmesan for topping

1. Proof the yeast by mixing it with the warm water. Let sit for 10 minutes until foamy.

2. In a bowl, combine the flour, salt, oregano, thyme, and basil, and stir into yeast mix. Stir to combine well. Stir in the garlic. Transfer to a lightly floured surface and knead the dough until it loses its stickiness, adding more flour as needed, about 10 minutes.

3. Coat the bottom and sides of a large mixing bowl (ceramic is best) with olive oil. Place the ball of dough in the bowl, cover loosely with plastic wrap, put it in a naturally warm, draft-free location, and let it rise until doubled in size, about 45 minutes to 1 hour.

4. Preheat the oven to 450 degrees.

5. Put a tablespoon of olive oil in the skillet, and press the dough into it. Drizzle some olive oil over it and sprinkle with salt and pepper, then with Parmesan cheese. Cover loosely with plastic wrap and let rise for about 20 minutes.

6. Put in the middle of the oven and bake for 25 to 30 minutes until golden and hot. Remove from oven and let rest for 5 minutes before removing from skillet to cool further.

ROSEMARY OLIVE FOCACCIA

SERVES 4 TO 6 ✦ ACTIVE TIME: 90 MINUTES ✦ START TO FINISH: 3 HOURS

This is another traditional flavor combination for focaccia. Be sure to use fresh rosemary, a combination of olives from an olive bar in a grocery or specialty store, and the red pepper flakes for a nice spicy heat. This is a great focaccia to serve with a large green salad for a summer lunch.

1 teaspoon active dry yeast

1 cup water (110 to 115 degrees)

2 to 2½ cups flour

1 teaspoon salt

1 tablespoon fresh rosemary leaves

1 teaspoon red pepper flakes

1 clove garlic, minced

½ cup olives, pitted and cut in half

3 tablespoons olive oil, plus more for drizzling over bread before baking

Sea salt (coarse grained) and freshly ground black pepper

1. Proof the yeast by mixing it with the warm water. Let sit for 10 minutes until foamy.

2. In a bowl, combine the flour, salt, rosemary, and red pepper flakes, and stir into yeast mix. Stir to combine well. Stir in the garlic and olives. Transfer to a lightly floured surface and knead the dough until it loses its stickiness, adding more flour as needed, about 10 minutes.

3. Coat the bottom and sides of a large mixing bowl (ceramic is best) with olive oil. Place the ball of dough in the bowl, cover loosely with plastic wrap, put it in a naturally warm, draft-free location, and let it rise until doubled in size, about 45 minutes to 1 hour.

4. Preheat the oven to 450 degrees.

5. Put a tablespoon of olive oil in the skillet, and press the dough into it. Drizzle some olive oil over it and sprinkle with salt and pepper. Cover loosely with plastic wrap and let rise for about 20 minutes.

6. Put in the middle of the oven and bake for 25 to 30 minutes until golden and hot. Remove from oven and let rest for 5 minutes before removing from skillet to cool further.

CARAMELIZED ONION AND LEEK FOCACCIA

SERVES 4 TO 6 ✦ ACTIVE TIME: 2 HOUR ✦ START TO FINISH: 3 HOURS

I'm a sucker for caramelized onions, which are onions that have been sautéed in butter and oil until soft and browned. They lose their bite, transformed instead into something almost sweet. The combination of leeks with the onions makes for a more subtle and even slightly sweeter topping.

8 tablespoons (1 stick) butter

3 tablespoons olive oil

1 medium yellow onion, peeled and sliced into thin slices

1 large leek, white and light green part only, sliced thin and rinsed of any sand

1 teaspoon active dry yeast

1 cup water (110 to 115 degrees)

2 to 2½ cups flour

1 teaspoon salt

1 teaspoon freshly ground black pepper

Sea salt (coarse grained)

Grated Parmesan for topping

1. In a skillet (cast-iron or otherwise), melt butter and 2 tablespoons of oil over medium-low heat. When melted, add the onion and leek slices. Increase the heat to medium-high and cook, stirring, until onions and leeks start to soften, about 5 minutes. Reduce heat to low and allow to cook, stirring occasionally, until cooked down and browned, about 10 to 15 minutes. Set aside.

2. Proof the yeast by mixing it with the warm water. Let sit for 10 minutes until foamy.

3. Combine the flour, salt, and pepper, and stir into yeast mix. Stir to combine well. Dough will be sticky. Transfer to a floured surface and knead the dough until it loses its stickiness, adding more flour as needed, about 10 minutes.

4. Coat the bottom and sides of a large mixing bowl (ceramic is best) with olive oil. Place the ball of dough in the bowl, cover loosely with plastic wrap, put it in a naturally warm, draft-free location, and let it rise until doubled in size, about 45 minutes to 1 hour.

5. Preheat the oven to 450 degrees.

6. Put a tablespoon of olive oil in the skillet, and press the dough into it. Top with the caramelized onion/leek mix. Season generously with sea salt and pepper, then with Parmesan cheese. Cover loosely with plastic wrap and let rise for about 20 minutes.

7. Put in the middle of the oven and bake for 25 to 30 minutes until golden and hot. Remove from oven and let rest for 5 minutes before removing from skillet to cool further.

PITA BREAD

MAKES 16 PITAS ✦ ACTIVE TIME: 60 MINUTES ✦ START TO FINISH: 2 HOURS

And here's an easy recipe for another flatbread that originated in the Mediterranean region, purportedly ancient Greece, as the word itself is Greek—pektos—meaning solid or clotted. It is popular around the world, but especially in Middle Eastern countries.

1 packet active dry yeast (2¼ teaspoons)

2½ cups water (110 to 115 degrees)

3 cups flour

1 tablespoon olive oil

1 tablespoon salt

3 cups whole wheat flour

1. Proof the yeast by mixing with the warm water. Let sit for about 10 minutes until foamy.

2. In a large bowl, add the yeast mix into the regular flour and stir until it forms a stiff dough. Cover and let the dough rise for about 1 hour.

3. Add the oil and salt to the dough and stir in the whole wheat flour in ½-cup increments. When finished, the dough should be soft. Turn onto a lightly floured surface and knead it until it is smooth and elastic, about 10 minutes.

4. Coat the bottom and sides of a large mixing bowl (ceramic is best) with butter. Place the ball of dough in the bowl, cover loosely with plastic wrap, put it in a naturally warm, draft-free location, and let it rise until doubled in size, about 45 minutes to 1 hour.

5. On a lightly floured surface, punch down the dough and cut into 16 pieces. Put the pieces on a baking sheet and cover with a dish towel while working with individual pieces.

6. Roll out the pieces with a rolling pin until they are approximately 7 inches across. Stack them between sheets of plastic wrap.

7. Heat the skillet over high heat and lightly oil the bottom. Cook the individual pitas about 20 seconds on one side, then flip and cook for about a minute on the other side, until bubbles form. Turn again and continue to cook until the pita puffs up, another minute or so. Keep the skillet lightly oiled while processing, and store the pitas on a plate under a clean dish towel until ready to serve.

Pitas make delicious, somewhat chewy bread pockets that can be filled with just about anything. In summer, I like to smear the inside with fresh hummus, and top with chopped carrots, lettuce, tomatoes, and hot sauce. Make a grilled cheese sandwich by putting some butter, slices of Swiss cheese, slices of American cheese, and slices of tomatoes inside, wrapping the sandwich in foil, heating it inside the foil on the skillet or on a grill for about 5 minutes a side, then unwrapping it and lightly toasting it directly on the hot pan.

NAAN

MAKES 4 TO 8 SERVINGS (8 PIECES) ✦ **ACTIVE TIME: 60 MINUTES** ✦
START TO FINISH: 3 TO 4 HOURS

This is the bread that is traditionally served with Indian cuisine, from spicy to saucy. It's cooked in a tandoor (clay oven) in India, but the cast-iron skillet turns out a very good replication!

1½ teaspoons active dry yeast

½ tablespoon sugar

1 cup water (110 to 115 degrees)

3 cups all-purpose flour or 1½ cups all-purpose and 1½ cups whole wheat pastry flour

¼ teaspoon salt

1 teaspoon baking powder

½ cup plain yogurt

4 tablespoons unsalted butter

¼ cup olive oil

1. Proof the yeast by mixing it with the sugar and ½ cup of the warm water. Let sit for 10 minutes until foamy.

2. In a bowl, combine the flour, salt, baking powder, remaining water, and yeast mix. Stir to combine well. Add the yogurt and 2 tablespoons of the butter, melted, and stir to form a soft dough.

3. Transfer to a lightly floured surface and knead the dough until it is springy and elastic, about 10 minutes.

4. Coat the bottom and sides of a large mixing bowl (ceramic is best) with butter. Place the ball of dough in the bowl, cover loosely with plastic wrap, put it in a naturally warm, draft-free location, and let it rise until doubled in size, about 1 to 2 hours.

5. Punch down the dough. Lightly flour a work surface again, take out the dough and, using a rolling pin, make a circle with the dough and cut it into 8 slices (like a pie).

6. Heat the skillet over high heat until it is very hot (about 5 minutes). Working with individual pieces of dough, roll them out to soften the sharp edges and make the pieces look more like teardrops. Brush both sides with olive oil and, working one at a time, place the pieces in the skillet.

7. Cook for 1 minute, turn the dough with tongs, cover the skillet, and cook the other side for about a minute (no longer). Transfer cooked naan to a plate and cover with foil to keep warm while making the additional pieces. Serve warm.

Variations

❋ You can add herbs or spices to the dough or the pan to make naan with different flavors.

❋ Add ¼ cup chopped fresh parsley to the dough.

❋ Sprinkle the skillet lightly with cumin or coriander or turmeric (or a combination) before cooking the pieces of naan.

❋ Use a seasoned olive oil to brush the pieces before cooking—one with hot pepper flakes or roasted garlic.

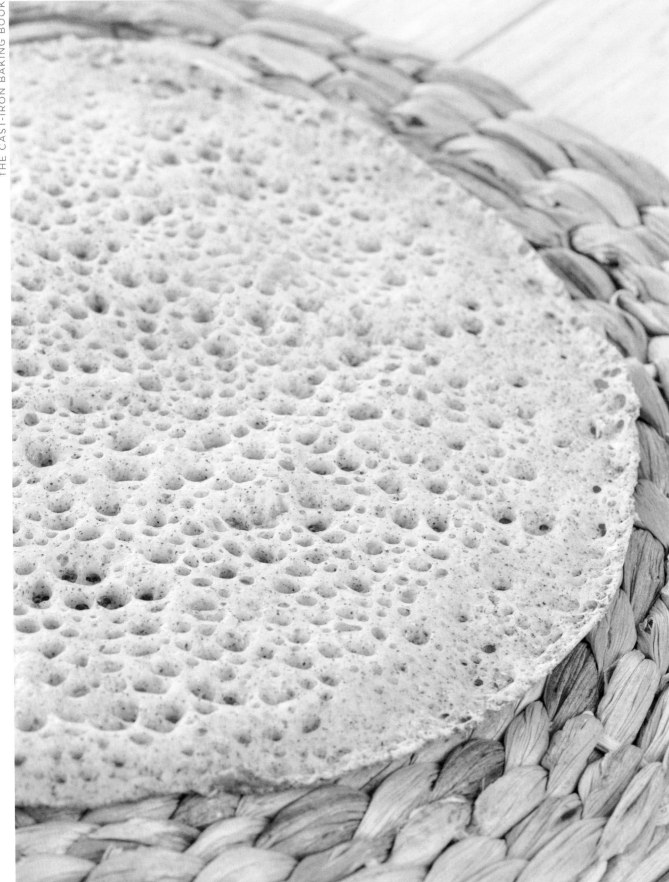

ETHIOPIAN INJERA

MAKES 1 INJERA ✦ ACTIVE TIME: 60 MINUTES ✦ START TO FINISH: 3 DAYS

If you've ever eaten at an Ethiopian restaurant, you'll remember that the centerpiece of the meal is the thick, spongy bread that's placed in the middle of the table. The dishes go around it, and you eat by ripping apart the bread and scooping up the other foods. I like to use it as almost a polenta or spongy pizza crust, topping with whatever leftovers I can combine to taste good. While the ingredients are minimal, you have to plan ahead for the day you want to serve the injera, as the "flour" needs to sit for several days to break down the grain.

½ teaspoon active
dry yeast

2 cups water
(110 to 115 degrees)

1½ cups ground teff
(put the seeds in a food
processor or blender
to reduce to "flour")

Salt

Vegetable oil

1. Proof the yeast by mixing with the warm water. Let sit for about 10 minutes until foamy.

2. Put the ground teff in a bowl and add the water/yeast. Mix thoroughly until a stiff dough forms. Put a dish towel over the bowl and stick it in a draft-free, fairly warm place in your kitchen. It will bubble and turn brown and smell sour. Let it sit for 2 to 3 days.

3. When ready to make the injera, add salt to the mix until some of the sour "bite" has dissipated. The mix at this time should resemble pancake batter.

4. Heat the skillet over medium heat and brush with vegetable oil. Pour enough batter on the pan to coat the bottom less than a pancake but more than a crepe. Tilt to spread the batter over the bottom of the skillet. Cook until holes form in the bread and the edges crisp up and lift away from the pan. The bread should not be flipped so be sure to let it cook thoroughly.

5. When cooked, lift it out with a spatula and put it on a plate or platter to cool. Place plastic wrap between injeras as you cook a batch of them. Serve warm with bowls of things like sautéed vegetables, grilled meat pieces, creamed spinach, sautéed mushrooms, or authentic Ethiopian dishes you can make— or Indian dishes you can find in grocery stores.

Thank goodness for Bob's Red Mill. They are bringing exotic grains from around the world to grocery stores here in the United States. One of those grains is teff, a wheat-like grain that's cultivated almost exclusively in Ethiopia. Teff is the smallest grain in the world, and it looks almost like poppy seeds (100 teff grains equal the size of a kernel of wheat!). It's full of iron, and it's gluten free. Bob's Red Mill website has recipes for teff, so you won't have to use the bag just to make injera—unless you want to.

PIZZA DOUGH

**SERVES 2 (ABOUT 4 LARGE SLICES) ✦ ACTIVE TIME: 30 MINUTES ✦
START TO FINISH: UP TO 3 DAYS**

*This is breadmaking at its simplest: flour, water, salt, and yeast. There's actually a cookbook
with that title! With this super-easy recipe, you can create amazing pizzas that can
be completely individualized with almost anything you have in the fridge or pantry, from
traditional cheese to "gourmet." And while the flavor will become more complex and
the crust crispier if you allow the dough to rise for a couple of hours (or up to 3 days
in the refrigerator), you can also roll it out and bake it within 15 minutes of making it.*

¾ cup water
(110 to 115 degrees)

1 teaspoon active
dry yeast

2 cups all-purpose
flour

1½ teaspoons salt

1 tablespoon olive oil

Toppings

**Traditional pizza
toppings include
the base of marinara
topped with mozzarella
cheese, as well as
ricotta cheese, Italian
seasonings, garlic,
fresh tomatoes,
pepperoni, sausage,
meatballs, spinach,
olives, mushrooms,
peppers, onions—
almost anything!**

1. If you'll be making pizza within the hour, preheat the oven to 450 degrees.

2. In a large bowl, add the warm water and yeast, stirring to dissolve the yeast.
Stir in the flour and salt and mix until the dough is just combined. It will
be sticky.

3. Turn out on a floured surface and start kneading until the flour is incorporated,
adding more if necessary until the dough is malleable and smooth, but
not overdone.

4. Allow the dough to rest for 15 minutes. While it's doing so, put the skillet
in the oven to get hot. Prepare the toppings for the pizza.

5. After 15 minutes or when ready, put a piece of parchment paper under
the dough. Start rolling and pushing it out to form a 9-inch disk that will fit
in the skillet. If it bounces back, let it rest before pushing or rolling it out again.

6. When the disk is formed, use pot holders or oven mitts to remove the skillet
from the oven. Add the olive oil and brush to distribute over the bottom.
Transfer the dough to the skillet and add the toppings.

7. Bake for 12 to 15 minutes until the crust starts to brown and the toppings
are hot and bubbling. Use caution taking the hot skillet from the oven.
Allow to cool for 5 minutes before lifting or sliding the pizza out and serving.

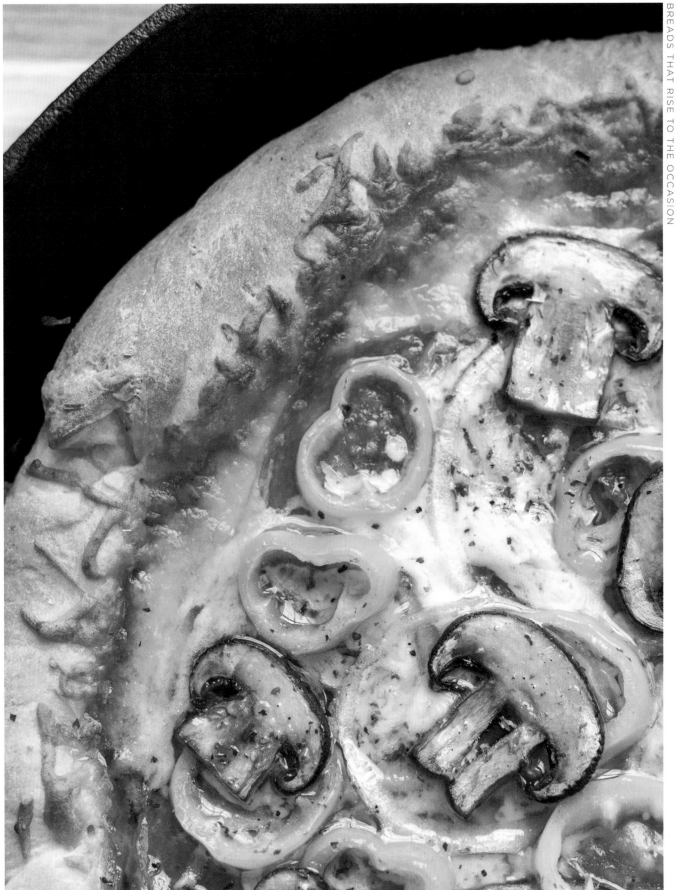

PALEO PIZZA DOUGH

SERVES 2 (ABOUT 4 LARGE SLICES) ✦ ACTIVE TIME: 30 MINUTES ✦
START TO FINISH: 30 MINUTES TO 3 DAYS

Paleo Bonus: You can make a great paleo-friendly pizza crust with that most wonderful of vegetables, cauliflower! Here's how:

1 head cauliflower

2 eggs, lightly beaten (or use just whites if you prefer)

1 tablespoon Italian seasoning

Salt and pepper to taste

1. Preheat the oven to 450 degrees.

2. Use a food processor to render the cauliflower florets into a rice-like consistency.

3. Fill a large pot about ⅓ full of water, bring to a boil, and cook the cauliflower in it until soft, about 5 minutes. Allow to drain thoroughly, then transfer cooked cauliflower to a clean dish towel and squeeze out as much water as possible. Put the cooked, dried cauliflower in a bowl.

4. Add the eggs, Italian seasoning, and salt and pepper to taste and mix thoroughly.

5. Take enough of the "dough" and, on a piece of parchment paper, shape it into a circle that will fit in the skillet. Lightly grease the skillet with coconut oil. Use a spatula and carefully transfer the crust to the skillet. Bake for about 10 minutes, until golden. Remove from the oven, allow to cool slightly, add toppings and bake again for 10 to 12 minutes.

WHOLE WHEAT PIZZA DOUGH

BREADS THAT RISE TO THE OCCASION

WHOLE WHEAT PIZZA DOUGH

SERVES 2 (ABOUT 4 LARGE SLICES) • ACTIVE TIME: 30 MINUTES
START TO FINISH: 30 MINUTES TO 3 DAYS

If you like an earthier-tasting crust with the added health benefits of whole wheat, this is another easy recipe to follow. Because pizza dough needs to be elastic, it's best to keep some of the regular flour in the blend. The honey helps activate the yeast, and mellows the whole wheat flavor just a bit.

¾ cup water
(110 to 115 degrees)

½ teaspoon honey

1 teaspoon active
dry yeast

1½ cups wheat flour

½ cup all-purpose
flour

1½ teaspoons salt

1 tablespoon olive oil

1. If you'll be making pizza within the hour, preheat the oven to 450 degrees.

2. In a large bowl, add the warm water, honey, and yeast, stirring to dissolve the yeast. Stir in the flours and salt and mix until the dough is just combined. It will be sticky.

3. Turn out on a floured surface and start kneading until the flour is incorporated, adding more if necessary until the dough is malleable and smooth, but not overdone.

4. Allow the dough to rest for 15 minutes. While it's doing so, put the skillet in the oven to get hot. Prepare the toppings for the pizza.

5. After 15 minutes or when ready, put a piece of parchment paper under the dough. Start rolling and pushing it out to form a 9-inch disk that will fit in the skillet. If it bounces back, let it rest before pushing or rolling it out again.

6. When the disk is formed, use pot holders or oven mitts to remove the skillet from the oven. Add the olive oil and brush to distribute over the bottom. Transfer the dough to the skillet and add the toppings.

7. Bake for 12 to 15 minutes until the crust starts to brown and the toppings are hot and bubbling. Use caution taking the hot skillet from the oven. Allow to cool for 5 minutes before lifting or sliding the pizza out and serving.

GARLIC KNOTS

MAKES ABOUT 3 DOZEN ✦ ACTIVE TIME: 45 MINUTES ✦ START TO FINISH: 90 MINUTES

Use the pizza dough recipe to make the knots themselves. They'll get that great cast-iron crust when they bake, then they can be bathed with garlic-parsley butter and put on a plate. Don't expect them to hang around for long, which is why this is a double batch of dough.

For the Knots

1½ cups water
(110 to 115 degrees)

2 teaspoons active
dry yeast

4 cups all-purpose
flour

2 teaspoons salt

1 tablespoon olive oil

Garlic-Parsley Sauce

8 tablespoons (1 stick)
unsalted butter

8 cloves garlic, minced

⅓ cup parsley leaves,
finely chopped

2 teaspoons salt

Grated Parmesan
if desired

1. In a large bowl, add the warm water and yeast, stirring to dissolve the yeast. Stir in the flour and salt and mix until the dough is just combined. It will be sticky.

2. Turn out on a floured surface and start kneading until the flour is incorporated, adding more if necessary until the dough is malleable and smooth, but not overdone.

3. Lightly grease a bowl and put the dough in it. Allow to rise for about an hour. Preheat the oven to 450 degrees.

4. Transfer to a lightly floured surface and push and stretch the dough into a large rectangle. If it resists, let it rest before stretching it further. Cut the rectangle into strips, and tie the strips into knots. Spread the tablespoon of olive oil over the bottom of the skillet. Tuck the knots into the skillet so there's just enough room separating them. Bake for about 15 minutes until golden brown.

5. While the knots are baking, prepare the garlic-parsley sauce. In a saucepan on medium heat, melt the butter. Add the garlic and reduce the heat to medium-low. Allow to cook, stirring occasionally, for about 3 minutes. This takes some of the pungency out of the garlic and also infuses the butter with the flavor. Stir in the chopped parsley and salt.

6. When the garlic knots come out of the oven, use a tea towel over your hand to pull them off the skillet and put them in a large mixing bowl. Scoop a large spoonful of the garlic-parsley sauce over the knots and toss to coat, adding a bit more if necessary. Use another spoon to transfer the coated knots to a plate. Sprinkle with Parmesan if desired and serve.

7. Continue to work in batches in the skillet until the dough is used up, or save some of the dough in the refrigerator for up to 3 days. The sauce can also be refrigerated for several days and reheated.

SAUSAGE CALZONE

SERVES 4 TO 6 ✦ ACTIVE TIME: 1 HOUR ✦ START TO FINISH: 2 HOURS

If you're looking for a meal that's more filling than just pizza, go for a calzone. Typically it's pizza dough folded over a filling into a half-moon shape. When made in a cast-iron skillet it's a double-crusted pizza. This allows for more filling to be piled inside, and as always with the cast-iron experience, the resulting dish will have a lovely bottom crust.

For the Dough

1½ cups water
(110 to 115 degrees)

2 teaspoons active
dry yeast

4 cups all-purpose
flour

2 teaspoons salt

For the Filling

1 tablespoon olive oil

1 pound sweet or
hot Italian sausage,
casing removed

2 cloves garlic,
pressed

½ teaspoon dried
oregano

½ teaspoon dried
thyme

Salt and pepper
to taste

½ cup marinara
sauce

2 cups shredded
mozzarella

Other filling ingredients
as desired

1. Make the dough by combining the warm water and yeast in a large bowl, stirring to dissolve the yeast. Stir in the flour and salt and mix until the dough is just combined. It will be sticky.

2. Turn out on a floured surface and start kneading until the flour is incorporated, adding more if necessary until the dough is malleable and smooth, but not overdone.

3. Lightly grease a bowl and put the dough in it. Allow to rise while you prepare the filling and preheat the oven, about 30 minutes.

4. Preheat the oven to 400 degrees.

5. Make the filling. In a large skillet over medium-high heat, cook the sausage in the olive oil, breaking up the meat into smaller pieces as it cooks. Stir continuously as it cooks, keeping the meat from sticking to the pan and making sure it is cooked evenly. Cook until the meat is no longer pink, about 15 minutes. Drain any excess fat. Reduce the heat to low and stir in the garlic and herbs. Season with salt and pepper. Set aside but do not refrigerate.

6. On a lightly floured surface, turn out the dough and separate it into two equal pieces. Roll each piece into a 12-inch circle.

7. Place one circle in the skillet. The dough should extend about half way up the side. Spread the marinara sauce over it, then add the cooked sausage, and top with the grated cheese. Place the other dough circle over the filling and crimp to seal the edges together with your fingers. Cut 4 slits in the top.

8. Bake for 25 minutes until the crust is a lovely golden brown. Use pot holders or oven mitts to remove the skillet. Allow to cool for about 10 minutes before slicing and serving. Serve with additional marinara sauce if desired.

SAUSAGE, PEPPER, AND ONION CALZONE

SERVES 4 TO 6 ✦ ACTIVE TIME: 1 HOUR ✦ START TO FINISH: 2 HOURS

Eating one of these is like being at an Italian street fair. Load it up so that the ingredients and juices overflow the crust when you eat it. Fabuloso!

For the Dough

1½ cups water
(110 to 115 degrees)

2 teaspoons active
dry yeast

4 cups all-purpose
flour

2 teaspoons salt

For the Filling

3 tablespoons olive oil

1 medium onion, sliced

3 cloves garlic, minced

1 pound hot Italian
sausage, sliced into
thin rounds

1 teaspoon red pepper
flakes (optional)

1 green pepper, seeds
removed, sliced into
strips

1 red pepper, seeds
removed, sliced into
strips

½ teaspoon oregano

Salt and pepper to taste

2 cups shredded
mozzarella

1. Make the dough by combining the warm water and yeast in a large bowl, stirring to dissolve the yeast. Stir in the flour and salt and mix until the dough is just combined. It will be sticky.

2. Turn out on a floured surface and start kneading until the flour is incorporated, adding more if necessary until the dough is malleable and smooth, but not overdone.

3. Lightly grease a bowl and put the dough in it. Allow to rise while you prepare the filling and preheat the oven, about 30 minutes.

4. Preheat the oven to 400 degrees.

5. Make the filling. In a large skillet over medium-high heat, cook the onions and garlic in the oil for about 2 minutes. Add the sausage slices and continue cooking until browned, another 5 minutes. Reduce the heat to medium, add the pepper slices, and stir to combine. Reduce the heat to low and continue cooking, stirring occasionally, until the pepper slices have softened and caramelized slightly in the oil, 10 to 15 minutes. Season with oregano, salt and pepper. Set aside but do not refrigerate.

6. On a lightly floured surface, turn out the dough and separate it into two equal pieces. Roll each piece into a 12-inch circle.

7. Place one circle in the skillet. The dough should extend about half way up the side. Spread the sausage and peppers over it, then top with the grated cheese. Place the other dough circle over the filling and crimp to seal the edges together with your fingers. Cut 4 slits in the top.

8. Bake for 25 minutes until the crust is a lovely golden brown. Use pot holders or oven mitts to remove the skillet. Allow to cool for about 10 minutes before slicing and serving. Serve with marinara sauce if desired.

PHILLY CHEESESTEAK CALZONE

SERVES 4 TO 6 ✦ ACTIVE TIME: 1 HOUR ✦ START TO FINISH: 2 HOURS

If you want to be a hero for the meat-loving men in your household, serve up one of these. With the hot, crispy crusts, the experience may even exceed a Philly cheesesteak sandwich. Super Bowl party at your house!

For the Dough

1½ cups water
(110 to 115 degrees)

2 teaspoons active
dry yeast

4 cups all-purpose
flour

2 teaspoons salt

For the Filling

2 tablespoons olive oil

1 medium onion,
sliced

1 package frozen
sliced steaks

2 cups shredded
American cheese
(do not substitute)

Salt and pepper to taste

1 jar marinara sauce,
heated

1. Make the dough by combining the warm water and yeast in a large bowl, stirring to dissolve the yeast. Stir in the flour and salt and mix until the dough is just combined. It will be sticky.

2. Turn out on a floured surface and start kneading until the flour is incorporated, adding more if necessary until the dough is malleable and smooth, but not overdone.

3. Lightly grease a bowl and put the dough in it. Allow to rise while you prepare the filling and preheat the oven, about 30 minutes.

4. Preheat the oven to 400 degrees.

5. Make the filling. Put the olive oil in a large skillet over medium-high heat and add the onion. Cook, stirring, so that the onions soften and caramelize, about 5 to 8 minutes. Transfer the onions to a bowl. Following the package instructions, cook the sliced steaks, transferring the cooked pieces to a plate until all are done.

6. On a lightly floured surface, turn out the dough and separate it into two equal pieces. Roll each piece into a 12-inch circle.

7. Place one circle in the skillet. The dough should extend about half way up the side. Spread the steaks over the dough, season with salt and pepper, then distribute the cheese over the meat and top with the cooked onions. Place the other dough circle over the filling and crimp to seal the edges together with your fingers. Cut 4 slits in the top.

8. Bake for 25 minutes until the crust is a lovely golden brown. Use pot holders or oven mitts to remove the skillet. Allow to cool for about 10 minutes before slicing and serving. Serve with warmed marinara sauce on the side.

BARBECUED CHICKEN AND PEPPERONI CALZONE

SERVES 4 TO 6 ✦ ACTIVE TIME: 1 HOUR ✦ START TO FINISH: 2 HOURS

Using leftover barbecued chicken gives this calzone recipe an added layer of tang, but you can use plain cooked chicken, too. Either will delight when brought out of the oven.

For the Dough

1½ cups water
(110 to 115 degrees)

2 teaspoons active
dry yeast

4 cups all-purpose
flour

2 teaspoons salt

For the Filling

1 cup marinara sauce

2 cloves garlic,
pressed

3 cups cooked
barbequed chicken,
cut into dice

1 cup pepperoni
slices

Salt and pepper
to taste

2 cups shredded
mozzarella cheese

Grated Parmesan

1. Make the dough by combining the warm water and yeast in a large bowl, stirring to dissolve the yeast. Stir in the flour and salt and mix until the dough is just combined. It will be sticky.

2. Turn out on a floured surface and start kneading until the flour is incorporated, adding more if necessary until the dough is malleable and smooth, but not overdone.

3. Lightly grease a bowl and put the dough in it. Allow to rise while you prepare the filling and preheat the oven, about 30 minutes.

4. Preheat the oven to 400 degrees.

5. Make the filling. In a large skillet over medium heat, warm the marinara sauce. Add the garlic and cook for a couple of minutes. Add the chicken pieces, stir, then add the pepperoni slices. Season with salt and pepper. Reduce the heat to low and simmer, uncovered, until ready to use.

6. On a lightly floured surface, turn out the dough and separate it into two equal pieces. Roll each piece into a 12-inch circle.

7. Place one circle in the skillet. The dough should extend about half way up the side. Spread the chicken/pepperoni mix evenly over the dough, then cover with the mozzarella and sprinkle with the Parmesan. Place the other dough circle over the filling and crimp to seal the edges together with your fingers. Cut 4 slits in the top.

8. Bake for 20 to 25 minutes until the crust is a lovely golden brown. Use pot holders or oven mitts to remove the skillet. Allow to cool for about 10 minutes before slicing and serving.

CHICKEN AND PESTO CALZONE

SERVES 4 TO 6 ✦ ACTIVE TIME: 1 HOUR ✦ START TO FINISH: 2 HOURS

Calzones are great pockets in which to stuff leftovers and create something yummy and different at the same time.

For the Dough

1½ cups water (110 to 115 degrees)

2 teaspoons active dry yeast

4 cups all-purpose flour

2 teaspoons salt

For the Filling

3 cups cooked chicken, diced

1 cup pesto

2 cups shredded mozzarella cheese

Grated Parmesan

1. Make the dough by combining the warm water and yeast in a large bowl, stirring to dissolve the yeast. Stir in the flour and salt and mix until the dough is just combined. It will be sticky.

2. Turn out on a floured surface and start kneading until the flour is incorporated, adding more if necessary until the dough is malleable and smooth, but not overdone.

3. Lightly grease a bowl and put the dough in it. Allow to rise while you preheat the oven, about 30 minutes.

4. Preheat the oven to 400 degrees.

5. On a lightly floured surface, turn out the dough and separate it into two equal pieces. Roll each piece into a 12-inch circle.

6. Place one circle in the skillet. The dough should extend about half way up the side. Spread the cooked chicken evenly over the dough, then dollop with the pesto. Sprinkle the mozzarella over everything, and then sprinkle with the Parmesan. Place the other dough circle over the filling and crimp to seal the edges together with your fingers. Cut 4 slits in the top.

7. Bake for 20 to 25 minutes until the crust is a lovely golden brown. Use pot holders or oven mitts to remove the skillet. Allow to cool for about 10 minutes before slicing and serving.

Variation

Make this a Buffalo Chicken and Pesto Calzone. When making the filling, put the cooked chicken pieces in a small bowl and add ¼ cup Frank's Hot Sauce. Stir to coat and drain any extra. Proceed to fill the calzone as directed above.

EGGPLANT, OLIVES, ONIONS, AND ANCHOVIES CALZONE

SERVES 4 TO 6 ✦ ACTIVE TIME: 1 HOUR ✦ START TO FINISH: 2 HOURS

Here's a calzone inspired by the flavors of Greece. For a clean, just-right taste, use anchovies marinated in oil, not anchovy paste, which is too salty and can be somewhat bitter.

For the Dough

1½ cups water
(110 to 115 degrees)

2 teaspoons active
dry yeast

4 cups all-purpose
flour

2 teaspoons salt

For the Filling

3 tablespoons olive oil

1 small eggplant,
cubed

3 garlic cloves,
minced

½ teaspoon red
pepper flakes

4 to 6 anchovy fillets
in oil (not anchovy
paste)

½ cup pitted black
olives, cut in half

2 cups shredded
mozzarella cheese

Grated Parmesan

1. Make the dough by combining the warm water and yeast in a large bowl, stirring to dissolve the yeast. Stir in the flour and salt and mix until the dough is just combined. It will be sticky.

2. Turn out on a floured surface and start kneading until the flour is incorporated, adding more if necessary until the dough is malleable and smooth, but not overdone.

3. Lightly grease a bowl and put the dough in it. Allow to rise while you prepare the filling and preheat the oven, about 30 minutes.

4. Preheat the oven to 400 degrees.

5. Make the filling. In a large skillet, heat 1 tablespoon of oil over medium-high heat. Add the eggplant cubes and cook, stirring, until softened and browned, about 6 to 8 minutes. Use a slotted spoon and transfer the pieces to a plate covered with a paper towel to absorb extra oil. Add 2 tablespoons of oil to the hot pan and add the garlic and red pepper flakes. Cook until the garlic bits dance in the oil, about 2 minutes. Add the anchovy fillets and the olives and stir to combine, cooking for an additional minute or two. Add the eggplant pieces and combine.

6. On a lightly floured surface, turn out the dough and separate it into two equal pieces. Roll each piece into a 12-inch circle.

7. Place one circle in the skillet. The dough should extend about half way up the side. Spread the eggplant/olive mixture evenly over the dough, then sprinkle the mozzarella over everything. Place the other dough circle over the filling and crimp to seal the edges together with your fingers. Cut 4 slits in the top.

8. Bake for 20 to 25 minutes until the crust is a lovely golden brown. Use pot holders or oven mitts to remove the skillet. Allow to cool for about 10 minutes before slicing and serving with grated Parmesan cheese.

KALE AND MONTEREY JACK CALZONE

SERVES 4 TO 6 ✦ ACTIVE TIME: 1 HOUR ✦ START TO FINISH: 2 HOURS

Kale, like spinach, holds up well when sautéed. You can use all kale in this recipe, or you can substitute other substantial leafy greens, like spinach, Swiss chard, beet tops, or arugula. The Monterey Jack has a hint of heat, but if you want something milder, use mozzarella.

For the Dough

1½ cups water
(110 to 115 degrees)

2 teaspoons active
dry yeast

4 cups all-purpose
flour

2 teaspoons salt

For the Filling

2 tablespoons olive oil

3 cloves garlic,
minced

1 pound fresh kale,
woody stems removed
and roughly chopped

Salt and pepper
to taste

2 cups grated Monterey
Jack cheese

1 egg, lightly beaten

½ cup grated
Parmesan cheese

1. Make the dough by combining the warm water and yeast in a large bowl, stirring to dissolve the yeast. Stir in the flour and salt and mix until the dough is just combined. It will be sticky.

2. Turn out on a floured surface and start kneading until the flour is incorporated, adding more if necessary until the dough is malleable and smooth, but not overdone.

3. Lightly grease a bowl and put the dough in it. Allow to rise while you prepare the filling and preheat the oven, about 30 minutes.

4. Preheat the oven to 400 degrees.

5. Make the filling. Put the olive oil and garlic in a large skillet over medium-high heat. Add the kale and sauté, stirring, until the kale is wilted, about 5 minutes. Reduce the heat to low and cover, stirring occasionally, until the kale is soft, another 5 to 10 minutes. Season with salt and pepper. Set aside but do not refrigerate. In a bowl, mix together the Monterey Jack, egg, and Parmesan cheese. Add the kale and stir to combine.

6. On a lightly floured surface, turn out the dough and separate it into two equal pieces. Roll each piece into a 12-inch circle.

7. Place one circle in the skillet. The dough should extend about half way up the side. Spread the kale mix evenly over the dough. Sprinkle with additional Parmesan cheese if desired. Place the other dough circle over the filling and crimp to seal the edges together with your fingers. Cut 4 slits in the top.

8. Bake for 20 to 25 minutes until the crust is a lovely golden brown. Use pot holders or oven mitts to remove the skillet. Allow to cool for about 10 minutes before slicing and serving.

SPINACH AND RICOTTA CALZONES

SERVES 4 TO 6 ✦ ACTIVE TIME: 1 HOUR ✦ START TO FINISH: 2 HOURS

Such a great combination! The resulting pizza "pie" is gooey with cheese and plenty of lovely green spinach. I like to spice this up with hot pepper flakes, but you can serve them on the side if you prefer.

For the Dough

1½ cups water
(110 to 115 degrees)

2 teaspoons active
dry yeast

4 cups all-purpose
flour

2 teaspoons salt

For the Filling

2 tablespoons olive oil

3 cloves garlic, minced

1 teaspoon red pepper
flakes (optional)

1 (16-oz.) package
frozen chopped
spinach leaves

Salt and pepper
to taste

2 cups fresh ricotta
cheese

1 egg, lightly beaten

½ cup grated Parmesan
cheese

1. Make the dough by combining the warm water and yeast in a large bowl, stirring to dissolve the yeast. Stir in the flour and salt and mix until the dough is just combined. It will be sticky.

2. Turn out on a floured surface and start kneading until the flour is incorporated, adding more if necessary until the dough is malleable and smooth, but not overdone.

3. Lightly grease a bowl and put the dough in it. Allow to rise while you prepare the filling and preheat the oven, about 30 minutes.

4. Preheat the oven to 400 degrees.

5. Make the filling. Put the olive oil, garlic, and red pepper flakes in a large skillet over medium-high heat and add the frozen spinach. Stir while cooking as the spinach thaws, coating the leaves with the oil and garlic, about 5 minutes. Reduce the heat to medium-low and cover, stirring occasionally, until the spinach is cooked through, another 15 minutes. Season with salt and pepper. Set aside but do not refrigerate. In a bowl, mix together the ricotta, egg, and Parmesan cheese.

6. On a lightly floured surface, turn out the dough and separate it into two equal pieces. Roll each piece into a 12-inch circle.

7. Place one circle in the skillet. The dough should extend about half way up the side. Spread the cooked spinach evenly over the dough, then dollop with the ricotta cheese mix. Use a spatula or the back of a large spoon to distribute the ricotta. Place the other dough circle over the filling and crimp to seal the edges together with your fingers. Cut 4 slits in the top.

8. Bake for 25 minutes until the crust is a lovely golden brown. Use pot holders or oven mitts to remove the skillet. Allow to cool for about 10 minutes before slicing and serving.

PEPPERONI BREAD

SERVES 6 TO 8 ✦ ACTIVE TIME: 60 MINUTES ✦ START TO FINISH: 3 HOURS

This is a favorite during football season, when the game hasn't actually started until this makes an appearance in front of the TV. Start in the morning for an afternoon game, as the dough needs to rise several times. But it's so delicious!

1¼ cups water
(110 to 115 degrees)

1 tablespoon sugar

1 oz. active dry yeast

1 tablespoon melted butter

1½ teaspoons salt

3½ cups flour

Salt and pepper

½ pound pepperoni, slivered

2 cups grated mozzarella cheese

1 teaspoon hot pepper flakes

1 teaspoon dried oregano

1 teaspoon garlic powder

1. Proof the yeast by mixing it with the water and sugar in a large bowl and then adding the yeast, stirring. Let sit until foamy, about 10 minutes. Add the salt and about half the flour to form a sticky dough. Cover the bowl with plastic wrap or a clean dish towel and let rise in a warm, draft-free place until it is double in size, about 1 hour.

2. Punch down the dough and add more flour to make it less sticky. Transfer to a floured surface and work the dough until it's smooth and elastic. Transfer to a lightly greased bowl and let sit for about 15 minutes.

3. On the floured surface, roll the dough out into a rectangle about 14x16 inches. Sprinkle with salt and pepper, spread the dough with pieces of pepperoni, then cheese, and top with a sprinkling of hot pepper flakes, oregano, and garlic powder. Roll up like a jellyroll, pinching the ends to secure filling.

4. Grease the skillet with the butter and lay the roll in it in a circle, working from the edges toward the center. Cover with a clean dish towel and let it rise again for about 1 hour. Preheat the oven to 375 degrees.

5. Bake the pepperoni bread for about 30 minutes, until golden on top and bubbling in the center. Serve immediately.

Variation

It's easy to make this into a full-blown **Meat Lover's Bread**. In addition to the pepperoni, add about ¼ to ½ cup of any or each of diced pancetta, diced smoked ham, crumbled cooked bacon, sautéed sausage, or diced cooked mini meatballs.

CORNBREAD, QUICHE & OTHERS

Before cast-iron made a comeback fairly recently (thank goodness!), the only way many of us saw it being used was for cornbread. Restaurants that specialized in barbeque would often serve cornbread in small cast-iron skillets. Cornbread has a natural association with cast-iron, so it seemed right to give it its own chapter. The other kind of things that are simple and easy to make along the same lines are quiches, frittatas, crepes, tortillas, and even Yorkshire pudding (a giant popover). You may find this one of the most popular chapters of the book for you.

CORNBREAD

SERVES 6 TO 8 ✦ ACTIVE TIME: 20 MINUTES ✦ START TO FINISH: 60 MINUTES

If you're going to make bread in a cast-iron skillet, you have to make cornbread! Many restaurants serve cornbread in a cast-iron skillet, which adds something to the flavor, if you ask me. No matter how you serve it, it tastes great.

2 cups finely ground yellow cornmeal

1 cup flour

¼ cup sugar

2 teaspoons baking powder

1 teaspoon baking soda

1 teaspoon salt

1½ cups milk

5 tablespoons unsalted butter, divided

2 eggs

1. Preheat the oven to 400 degrees.

2. In a large bowl, combine cornmeal, flour, sugar, baking powder, baking soda, and salt. Put ½ cup milk in a measuring cup. Add 2 tablespoons butter, cut into pieces. Put in the microwave and heat on high for 1 minute so that butter is melted into the milk. Pour this over the dry ingredients and begin stirring. Gradually add the additional cup of milk and stir, then add the eggs and continue stirring until thoroughly combined.

3. Heat the skillet over medium heat and melt the 3 remaining tablespoons of butter in it. Add the batter and shake the pan gently to evenly distribute.

4. Transfer the skillet to the oven and cook for 25 to 30 minutes, until light golden brown and a toothpick inserted in the middle comes out clean.

5. Using pot holders or oven mitts, remove the skillet from the oven and let the bread cool for 10 to 15 minutes before slicing and serving.

Cornbread recipes are as varied and plentiful as those for chili. A great way to discover different ones that you like without having to go through multiple cookbooks and lots of time in the kitchen yourself is to invite friends and family to a Cast-Iron Cornbread Cook-Off. Make the chili the way you like it (and plenty of it), then have people bring over their cornbreads with recipes.

CORNY-SPICY CORNBREAD

SERVES 6 TO 8 ✦ ACTIVE TIME: 25 MINUTES ✦ START TO FINISH: 60 MINUTES

Now that I've suggested the family or neighborhood cornbread challenge, I have to offer my own contender for first prize, since I love a cornbread that actually has kernels of corn in it. If you like spicy, toss in the jalapeños, too.

2 cups finely ground yellow cornmeal

1 cup flour

¼ cup sugar

2 teaspoons baking powder

1 teaspoon baking soda

1 teaspoon salt

1½ cups milk

4 tablespoons unsalted butter, divided

2 eggs

1 cup corn kernels (can be from fresh-cooked corn on the cob, or use canned being sure to drain the liquid)

¼ to ½ cup diced jalapeño peppers

1. Preheat the oven to 400 degrees.

2. In a large bowl, combine the cornmeal, flour, sugar, baking powder, baking soda, and salt. Put ½ cup milk in a measuring cup. Add the 2 tablespoons butter, cut into pieces. Put in the microwave and heat on high for 1 minute so that butter is melted into the milk. Pour this over the dry ingredients and begin stirring. Gradually add the additional cup of milk and stir, then add the eggs and continue stirring until thoroughly combined. When batter is mixed, fold in the corn kernels and jalapeños.

3. Heat the skillet over medium heat and melt the 2 remaining tablespoons of butter in it. Add the batter and shake the pan gently to evenly distribute.

4. Transfer the skillet to the oven and cook for 25 to 30 minutes, until light golden brown and a toothpick inserted in the middle comes out clean.

5. Using pot holders or oven mitts, remove the skillet from the oven and let the bread cool for 10 to 15 minutes before slicing and serving.

BACON CHEDDAR CORNBREAD

SERVES 6 TO 8 ✦ ACTIVE TIME: 20 MINUTES ✦ START TO FINISH: 60 MINUTES

The smoky-salty combination of bacon and cheddar are a perfect complement to so many foods—burgers, grilled cheese sandwiches, fried eggs—and now, cornbread. If you have a houseful of guys on a Sunday morning (especially if they're teenagers), whip this up and watch it disappear.

2 cups finely ground yellow cornmeal

1 cup flour

¼ cup sugar

2 teaspoons baking powder

1 teaspoon baking soda

1 teaspoon salt

1½ cups milk

4 tablespoons unsalted butter, divided

2 eggs

1 cup crunchy bacon bits

4 oz. (½ to ¾ cup) sharp cheddar cheese, grated

1. Preheat the oven to 400 degrees.

2. In a large bowl, combine the cornmeal, flour, sugar, baking powder, baking soda, and salt. Put ½ cup milk in a measuring cup. Add the 2 tablespoons butter, cut into pieces. Put in the microwave and heat on high for 1 minute so that butter is melted into the milk. Pour this over the dry ingredients and begin stirring. Gradually add the additional cup of milk, then add the eggs, and stir until thoroughly combined. When batter is mixed, fold in most of the bacon pieces and grated cheese, saving some to sprinkle on top.

3. Heat the skillet over medium heat and melt the 2 remaining tablespoons of butter in it. Add the batter and shake the pan gently to evenly distribute. Sprinkle the top with the extra bacon and cheese.

4. Transfer the skillet to the oven and cook for 25 to 30 minutes, until light golden brown and a toothpick inserted in the middle comes out clean.

5. Using pot holders or oven mitts, remove the skillet from the oven and let the bread cool for 10 to 15 minutes before slicing and serving.

CORN CHOWDER CORNBREAD

SERVES 6 TO 8 ✦ ACTIVE TIME: 20 MINUTES ✦ START TO FINISH: 60 MINUTES

I was going through my cans of soup one day and thought, "Why not use chicken corn chowder soup instead of milk in a cornbread recipe?" So I tried it. Super easy. Nice, moist result. And this leads, of course, to thoughts of other soups as flavor additives for cornbread. I'm sure you can think of some, too.

2 cups finely ground yellow cornmeal

1 cup flour

¼ cup sugar

2 teaspoons baking powder

1 teaspoon baking soda

1 teaspoon salt

1 teaspoon cayenne pepper (optional)

¼ cup milk

4 tablespoons unsalted butter, divided

1 (18.5-oz.) can of chicken corn chowder soup

2 eggs

1. Preheat the oven to 400 degrees.

2. In a large bowl, combine the cornmeal, flour, sugar, baking powder, baking soda, salt, and cayenne pepper. Put the ¼ cup milk in a measuring cup. Add the 2 tablespoons butter, cut into pieces. Put in the microwave and heat on high for 1 minute so that butter is melted into the milk. Pour this over the dry ingredients and begin stirring. Add the can of soup and stir, then add the eggs and continue stirring until thoroughly combined.

3. Heat the skillet over medium heat and melt the 2 remaining tablespoons of butter in it. Add the batter and shake the pan gently to evenly distribute.

4. Transfer the skillet to the oven and cook for 25 to 30 minutes, until light golden brown and a toothpick inserted in the middle comes out clean.

5. Using pot holders or oven mitts, remove the skillet from the oven and let the bread cool for 10 to 15 minutes before slicing and serving.

SIMPLY SENSATIONAL IRISH SODA BREAD

MAKES 1 LOAF ✦ ACTIVE TIME: 30 MINUTES ✦ START TO FINISH: 90 MINUTES

Make this on a weekend morning when you have some extra time, then have slices of it later in the day with a cup of coffee or tea.

4 cups flour

½ cup sugar

⅛ teaspoon salt

3¼ teaspoons baking powder

½ teaspoon baking soda

2 tablespoons caraway seeds

2 large eggs, lightly beaten

1½ cups buttermilk

8 oz. golden raisins

1. Preheat the oven to 450 degrees.

2. Combine the flour, sugar, salt, baking powder, baking soda, and caraway seeds. Add the beaten eggs and stir to combine. Gradually add the buttermilk until the dough is sticky and messy. Stir in the raisins.

3. Generously butter the skillet, and scoop and spread the dough in it.

4. Bake for about 1 hour, until the top is crusty and brown and the bread sounds hollow when tapped. Insert a toothpick in the center, too, to be sure the dough is cooked through. It should come out clean.

5. Serve with fresh butter and orange marmalade.

It wouldn't be St. Patrick's Day without Irish Soda bread. According to the Culinary Institute of America, "With a history spanning more than two centuries, soda bread is a traditional Irish specialty. The first loaf, consisting of little more than flour, baking soda, salt, and sour milk, made its debut in the mid-1800s when baking soda found its way into Irish kitchens." They don't mention the raisins or caraway seeds, but I consider these essential!

CHEESY CHIVE SODA BREAD

MAKES 1 LOAF ✦ ACTIVE TIME: 40 MINUTES ✦ START TO FINISH: 90 MINUTES

If you're looking for a savory version of a simple soda bread to serve with something like soup or stew, this is a great recipe.

3 cups white flour

2 cups spelt flour

¾ cup rolled oats (not instant)

2 tablespoons sugar

1 tablespoon baking powder

1 teaspoon salt

1 teaspoon baking soda

8 tablespoons (1 stick) butter, melted and cooled

2½ cups buttermilk

1 large egg, lightly beaten

¼ cup chopped chives

1¼ cups grated sharp white cheddar cheese

Freshly ground pepper

1. Preheat the oven to 350 degrees.

2. In a large bowl, combine the flours, oats, sugar, baking powder, salt, and baking soda. Whisk to combine thoroughly. In another bowl, combine the butter, buttermilk, and egg.

3. Add the milk mixture to the flour mixture and stir vigorously to blend. Dough will be sticky. Stir in the chives and 1 cup of the grated cheese.

4. Liberally grease the skillet with butter. Scoop and spread the dough into the skillet. Grate pepper over the top, then sprinkle the remaining cheese over it. Using a sharp knife, make an "x" in the center, about ½-inch deep, to settle the cheese further into the dough as it cooks.

5. Bake in the oven for about 1 hour and 15 minutes until golden on top and a toothpick inserted in the center comes out clean. Allow to sit in the skillet for a few minutes before serving.

Soda bread doesn't keep so well, so if you happen to have any left over, be sure to wrap it tightly in plastic wrap. Store it in the refrigerator. It will last for about 3 days this way. The bread makes great toast!

SPICY SHRIMP POLENTA

SERVES 4 TO 6 ✦ ACTIVE TIME: 30 MINUTES ✦ START TO FINISH: 60 MINUTES

If you're looking for a recipe for a fun cocktail party finger food, this is it—essentially a take on fish tacos but much easier to eat! Plus, it's naturally gluten-free!

3 tablespoons canola oil

½ pound small shrimp, thawed (if frozen), peeled, and cut in half

1 cup coarse-grind or medium-grind polenta

3 cups water

1 teaspoon horseradish

1 teaspoon hot pepper flakes

Salt and freshly ground black pepper

Fresh coriander for garnish

1. Preheat the oven to 400 degrees.

2. Heat the canola oil in a skillet over medium-high heat. When hot but not smoking, add the shrimp. Stirring constantly and with a light touch, sauté the shrimp until just pink, about 3 to 5 minutes. Remove the pan from the heat and use a slotted spoon to transfer the shrimp to a plate lined with paper towels. Keep the oil in the skillet.

3. In a heavy saucepan, whisk together the polenta and water. Heat over medium and bring to a boil, whisking to prevent lumps from forming. When bubbling, reduce the heat to low and simmer, uncovered, for a couple of minutes or until smooth. Remove from heat and stir in the horseradish and pepper flakes. Season with salt and black pepper. Taste the polenta to see if the horseradish is strong enough for you. If you think it could use more, add another ½ teaspoon but be careful not to overdo it. Stir in the shrimp.

4. Pour the polenta into the skillet, smoothing the surface with the back of a spoon. Put in the oven and bake for about 30 minutes, until it is lightly golden and coming away from the edges of the pan. Allow to cool for 5 to 10 minutes, then work quickly and carefully to invert the polenta cake onto a platter. Allow to cool to room temperature.

5. Cut the polenta into bite-sized pieces, and top each piece with a sprig of coriander. Serve immediately.

POLENTA CAKES WITH GREENS

SERVES 4 TO 6 ✦ ACTIVE TIME: 30 MINUTES ✦ START TO FINISH: 60 MINUTES

Polenta is cornmeal cooked into porridge and then baked or fried. It forms a lovely, bright yellow cake that is moist yet firm. It can be topped with all kinds of things, but in this recipe, it is the base for sautéed vegetables. Delicious!

Olive oil for preparing skillet

1 cup coarse-grind or medium-grind polenta

3 cups water

Salt and freshly ground black pepper

1 pound bitter greens such as kale, chard, escarole, or dandelion, tough stems removed

3 tablespoons extra virgin olive oil

3 cloves garlic, chopped

Red pepper flakes

Grated Romano for topping

1. Preheat the oven to 400 degrees.

2. Liberally oil the skillet and put it in the oven for a few minutes to heat.

3. In a heavy saucepan, whisk together the polenta and water. Heat over medium and bring to a boil, whisking to prevent lumps from forming. When bubbling, reduce the heat to low and simmer, uncovered, for a couple of minutes or until smooth. Season with salt and black pepper.

4. Pour the polenta into the skillet. Put in the oven and bake for about 30 minutes, until it is lightly golden and coming away from the edges of the pan.

5. While it's baking, make the greens. Bring a large pot of salted water to a boil, add the greens, and boil until very tender, 15 to 20 minutes. Drain in a colander and squeeze to remove excess moisture. Cut the greens into pieces. Heat the olive oil in a pan, add the garlic and cook, stirring, until fragrant, about 2 minutes. Add the red pepper flakes, stir, then add the greens. Cook until heated through. Season with salt and pepper. Keep warm until polenta is cooked.

6. Cut the polenta into wedges, top with greens, and sprinkle on the grated cheese.

Variation

Substitute ½ pound baby spinach leaves and ½ pound kale (tough stems removed) or Swiss chard (stems removed) for the pound of mixed greens.

POLENTA CAKE WITH MUSHROOMS AND ONIONS

SERVES 4 TO 6 ◆ ACTIVE TIME: 30 MINUTES ◆ START TO FINISH: 75 MINUTES

Think vegetarian Shepherd's Pie with this recipe—the mushrooms and onions are the "meat" and the polenta bakes on top the way a layer of mashed potatoes would. A cast-iron skillet seems a natural home for this kind of dish, which is hearty and rustic.

8 tablespoons (1 stick) butter

1 to 1½ cups thinly sliced onions

2 pounds mushrooms, stems removed and cut into pieces

1 teaspoon Worcestershire sauce

1 cup coarse-grind or medium-grind polenta

3 cups water

Salt and freshly ground black pepper

1. Preheat the oven to 400 degrees.

2. Melt 6 tablespoons of the butter in the skillet over medium heat. Add the onion slices and increase the heat to medium high. Sauté the onions until just soft, about 3 minutes. Add the mushroom pieces and continue to cook over medium-high heat, stirring frequently, until the mushrooms and onions are soft and reduced in volume, about 8 minutes. Stir in the Worcestershire sauce, and season with salt and pepper. Remove from the heat.

3. In a heavy saucepan, whisk together the polenta and water. Heat over medium and bring to a boil, whisking to prevent lumps from forming. When bubbling, reduce the heat to low and simmer, uncovered, for a couple of minutes or until smooth. Season with salt and black pepper.

4. Pour the polenta into the skillet, evenly over the mushroom/onion mixture, smoothing the surface with the back of a spoon. Cut the remaining 2 tablespoons of butter into thin pieces and dot the surface of the polenta with them.

5. Put in the oven and bake for 30 minutes, until it is lightly golden and coming away from the edges of the pan (the mushroom/onion mix should be bubbling hot). Allow to cool for 10 minutes before serving.

6. Cut the polenta into wedges. Serve immediately.

PERFECT PIE CRUSTS

MAKES 2 CRUSTS ✦ ACTIVE TIME: 15 MINUTES ✦ START TO FINISH: 75 MINUTES

Made in a cast-iron skillet, pie crust finishes to a lovely crispness. We'll use this recipe for a whole bunch of pies and quiches, though you always have the option of using store-bought crusts, if you're in a hurry.

2½ cups flour

1 teaspoon sugar

1 teaspoon salt

1 cup (2 sticks) unsalted butter, cut into small cubes

4 to 6 tablespoons very cold water

1. To make the crust, combine flour, sugar, and salt in a large bowl.

2. Using a pastry knife or a large fork, work the butter cubes into the flour mixture until the butter pieces are no larger than a pebble and the dough is crumbly.

3. Add the very cold water 2 tablespoons at a time and work the dough with your hands until it holds together. Form it into two pieces, wrap them in plastic wrap, and refrigerate for 1 hour before rolling out.

BROCCOLI-SWISS QUICHE

SERVES 6 TO 8 ✦ ACTIVE TIME: 30 MINUTES ✦ START TO FINISH: 60 MINUTES

A quiche is essentially a savory pie, and like any good pie, it can be so satisfying. There's something simple yet elegant about pie, and a quiche is no exception. This is a recipe that features broccoli paired with Swiss cheese and artichoke hearts, accented with Italian seasoning. It's delicious heated or at room temperature, and, served with a salad, makes a great meal.

1 homemade pie dough (see opposite page) or 1 pre-made refrigerator pie dough (14.01 oz)

1 teaspoon Dijon mustard

1¼ cup grated/shredded Swiss cheese

3 cups broccoli florets and stems, cooked but not too soft

6 eggs

¾ cup half-and-half

1 teaspoon salt

1 teaspoon Italian seasoning

½ teaspoon ground black pepper

1 (6-oz.) jar quartered, marinated artichoke hearts, drained

½ cup grated Parmesan cheese

1. Preheat the oven to 350 degrees.

2. Make homemade pie crust (page 146) or get out your store-bought refrigerated pie dough and roll it out if needed.

3. Brush the mustard over the bottom of the dough. Next, use about ¼ cup of the cheese and sprinkle it over the dough. Place the broccoli pieces in the pie.

4. In a large bowl, whisk the eggs, half-and-half, salt, Italian seasoning, and pepper together until combined. Add the remaining Swiss cheese and mix well.

5. Pour the egg mixture over the broccoli pieces, giving the skillet a gentle shake to distribute the liquid. Arrange artichoke hearts on top. Sprinkle the Parmesan over everything.

6. Put the skillet in the oven and bake for 35 to 40 minutes or until the quiche is puffy and golden brown and the eggs are set. Use pot holders or oven mitts to take the skillet out of the oven. Allow to sit for 10 minutes before slicing and serving.

QUICHE WITH SAUTÉED LEEKS

SERVES 6 TO 8 ✦ ACTIVE TIME: 30 MINUTES ✦ START TO FINISH: 60 MINUTES

The leeks in this recipe are sautéed until soft and golden, which brings out their delectable mild onion flavor. Swiss or gruyére cheese is the perfect complement. This is an easy-to-make quiche that is nonetheless quite elegant.

1 pre-made refrigerator pie dough (14.1 oz) or homemade pie dough (page 146)

3 large leeks, white and light green parts only

2 tablespoons olive oil

3 eggs

1 cup whole milk or half-and-half

½ to ¾ cup shredded Swiss or gruyére cheese

Salt and pepper to taste

1. Preheat the oven to 400 degrees.

2. Allow the refrigerated pie dough to come to room temperature. On a lightly floured surface, unroll and smooth it. Gently fold it and place in the skillet, pressing gently into place. Crimp the edges at the top of the skillet for a decorative touch.

3. Prepare the leeks by cutting the white and light green parts only into thin slices. Separate the rings in a colander, and rinse thoroughly to remove any sand or grit. Pat dry.

4. In another skillet, heat the olive oil over medium-high heat. Add the leeks and cook, stirring, for a minute or two. Lower the heat and continue to cook so that the leeks become tender and golden, not overly browned, about 10 to 15 minutes. Stir frequently.

5. In a large bowl, whisk the eggs and milk or half-and-half until thoroughly combined. Add the shredded cheese and season with salt and pepper. Stir.

6. Spread the sautéed leeks over the crust in the skillet. Pour the egg/cheese mixture over them.

7. Put the skillet in the oven and bake for about 30 minutes or until the quiche is puffy and golden brown and the eggs are set. Use pot holders or oven mitts to take the skillet out of the oven. Allow to sit for 10 minutes before slicing and serving.

QUICHE LORRAINE

SERVES 6 TO 8 ✦ **ACTIVE TIME: 30 MINUTES** ✦ **START TO FINISH: 60 MINUTES**

There's a reason this recipe has become a household name around the world: it's fabulous! Use heavy cream for a suppleness and richness that you can't get from half-and-half. It may be more fattening, but it's also more delicious. It seems like cheese should be added to this, but the classic French quiche Lorraine does not have it. Celebrate France when you eat this and enjoy with a glass of wine. Voilà!

1 pre-made refrigerator pie dough (14.1 oz) or homemade pie dough (page 146)

½ to ¾ pound thick-cut bacon, cut into ¼-inch pieces

3 large eggs

2 cups heavy cream

¾ teaspoon coarse salt

¼ teaspoon freshly ground pepper

1. Preheat the oven to 400 degrees.

2. Allow the refrigerated pie dough to come to room temperature. On a lightly floured surface, unroll and smooth it. Gently fold it and place in the skillet, pressing gently into place. Crimp the edges at the top of the skillet for a decorative touch.

3. Use a regular skillet or griddle to cook the bacon pieces, sautéing them until just crispy (don't overcook the bacon). The bacon will cook faster in pieces, so keep an eye on it. Transfer the pieces to a plate lined with a paper towel to absorb some of the grease.

4. In a large bowl, whisk the eggs and cream until thoroughly combined. Add the salt and pepper and stir.

5. Pour the egg mixture into the crust-lined skillet and sprinkle with the bacon pieces.

6. Put the skillet in the oven and bake for about 30 minutes or until the quiche is puffy and golden brown and the eggs are set. Use pot holders or oven mitts to take the skillet out of the oven. Allow to sit for 10 minutes before slicing and serving.

SMOKED SALMON AND DILL QUICHE

SERVES 6 TO 8 ✦ ACTIVE TIME: 30 MINUTES ✦ START TO FINISH: 60 MINUTES

Any good deli in New York City will serve smoked salmon for breakfast—typically on a bagel with a schmear of cream cheese, a few capers, and a sprig of dill. What a treat! Putting smoked salmon and dill in a quiche makes for a dish that is still fantastic for fans of the fish, but is mellower and therefore more palatable for those who might not be…though no one can resist.

1 pre-made refrigerator pie dough (14.1 oz) or homemade pie dough (page 146)

1 teaspoon Dijon mustard

1 pound smoked salmon, cut or torn into nickel-sized pieces

4 eggs

1 cup half-and-half

1 teaspoon salt

½ teaspoon ground black pepper

1 tablespoon dill, finely minced

1 (3-oz.) package cream cheese, cut into small cubes

1. Preheat the oven to 350 degrees.

2. Allow the refrigerated pie dough to come to room temperature. On a lightly floured surface, unroll and smooth it. Gently fold it and place in the skillet, pressing gently into place. Crimp the edges at the top of the skillet for a decorative touch.

3. Brush the mustard over the bottom of the dough. Place the salmon pieces in the pie.

4. In a large bowl, whisk the eggs, half-and-half, salt, and pepper together until combined. Add the dill and mix well.

5. Pour the egg mixture over the salmon pieces, giving the skillet a gentle shake to distribute the liquid. Sprinkle the cubes of cream cheese evenly on top.

6. Put the skillet in the oven and bake for 35 to 40 minutes or until the quiche is puffy and golden brown and the eggs are set. Use pot holders or oven mitts to take the skillet out of the oven. Allow to sit for 10 minutes before slicing and serving.

TOMATO-MUSHROOM FRITTATA

SERVES 4 ✦ **ACTIVE TIME: 20 MINUTES** ✦ **START TO FINISH: 40 MINUTES**

Frittatas are like omelets in that they are combinations of eggs with other ingredients. The difference is that the frittata is like a crustless quiche, where the extras are cooked in with the eggs instead of being placed on top of an egg "pancake" and folded over. This one is especially yummy. Plus, all of the frittatas in this baking book are naturally gluten-free!

2 tablespoons butter

6 eggs

¼ cup milk or heavy cream

½ pound mushroom pieces, cleaned and sliced

1 large tomato, core and seeds removed, cut into small pieces

½ teaspoon salt

Freshly ground black pepper

¼ cup basil, coarsely chopped

½ to 1 teaspoon hot sauce, if desired

1. Preheat the broiler to low.

2. Heat the skillet on medium-high heat. Melt the butter in the skillet, being careful not to let it burn.

3. Whisk the eggs in a large bowl until combined. Add the milk or cream and stir. Add the mushroom pieces and tomatoes. Add the salt and pepper, and the hot sauce if desired.

4. Pour the egg mixture into the skillet. After a couple of minutes, as the eggs begin to set, sprinkle the basil over them. Lower the heat to medium or low, cover, and finish cooking until eggs are set, another 10 minutes. Place the skillet under the broiler for just a couple of minutes to "toast" the top.

5. Allow to sit for a few minutes. Season with additional salt and pepper, and serve.

Paleo Variations

To make any of the frittatas in this baking book paleo-friendly, you'll need to substitute the butter and other dairy ingredients. Here are some great substitutes that will ensure flavor and consistency:

❋ Use ghee (clarified butter) or lard instead of butter at a 1:1 ratio

❋ Use coconut milk instead of milk or half-and-half

❋ Paleo-appropriate cheese is an oxymoron, as the quintessential ingredient in cheese is, of course, milk. The dairy-free cheeses you find in grocery stores are typically full of junk, which defeats the purpose healthy eating. You can add nutritional yeast for a cheesy flavor. Experiment with it, but a few tablespoons for a frittata is usually enough. Further, consider what the cheese is contributing. You can substitute avocado for a dense creaminess.

MAINLY MUSHROOM FRITTATA

SERVES 4 ✦ **ACTIVE TIME: 20 MINUTES** ✦ **START TO FINISH: 40 MINUTES**

If you love mushrooms (and I sure do!), you'll love this frittata. The mushrooms are moist and earthy, the perfect base for the Swiss cheese and eggs.

3 tablespoons butter

½ onion, diced

1 pound mushrooms, picked over and sliced or chopped

1 teaspoon salt

½ teaspoon pepper

1 tablespoon dry Vermouth (optional)

8 eggs

½ cup milk or half-and-half

1 cup Swiss cheese, shredded

⅓ cup fresh parsley, chopped

1. Melt the butter in the skillet over medium-high heat. Add the onions and cook, stirring, until translucent, about 3 minutes. Add the mushrooms, lower the heat slightly, and cook, stirring occasionally, until soft, 5 to 10 minutes. Drain the liquid from the pan. Season the mushrooms with the salt and pepper, and add the Vermouth if desired.

2. In a bowl, whisk the eggs with the milk. Pour the egg mixture over the mushrooms. Sprinkle the cheese all around the top, and then sprinkle the parsley over everything. Cover the skillet and let cook until set, about 10 minutes. Place the skillet in the oven under the broiler and "toast" the top, about 2 minutes.

The selection of mushrooms in grocery stores is getting bigger and bigger. You can use one kind of mushroom for this dish, or you can use several kinds together. For example, you could use sliced white mushrooms, and you won't need to do much prep work with them. Or you could choose Portobellos, which have a meatier texture and flavor. There are also shiitake or cremini mushrooms. If you mix the mushrooms, just be sure to cut them into similarly sized pieces so they cook evenly.

CORNBREAD, QUICHE & OTHERS

SPINACH FRITTATA

SERVES 4 ✦ ACTIVE TIME: 20 MINUTES ✦ START TO FINISH: 30 MINUTES

This delicious combination gives a nod to Greek cuisine with the addition of feta cheese. Serve this for brunch with other classic Greek foods, like olives, pita wedges, and tzatziki sauce (see recipe below).

6 eggs

2 tablespoons butter

¼ cup chopped red onion

1 clove garlic, minced

2 cups fresh spinach leaves, coarse stems removed, roughly chopped

½ cup feta cheese

Salt and pepper to taste

1. Preheat the broiler to low.

2. In a small bowl, beat the eggs with a whisk until combined.

3. Heat skillet over medium-high heat. Melt the butter in the skillet and add the onions and garlic, stirring to cook until onions are translucent, about 3 minutes.

4. Add the spinach and stir so the leaves wilt. Sprinkle the feta over the mixture.

5. Pour the eggs over everything and shake the pan to evenly distribute them. Sprinkle with salt and pepper. Cover the skillet and let cook until set, about 10 minutes. Place the skillet in the oven under the broiler to "toast" the top, about 2 minutes.

6. Allow to stand for a couple of minutes, and serve. Season with additional salt and pepper.

Tzatziki Sauce is a simple blend of cucumbers, yogurt, garlic, and lemon juice, and it's a refreshing accompaniment to egg and meat dishes. To make it, peel, remove the seeds from, and finely chop half of a cucumber. Wrap it in a cheesecloth or paper towel and squeeze it to get the juice out. Put the pieces in a bowl. Add 2 cups plain Greek yogurt, 2 tablespoons fresh-squeezed lemon juice, 4 cloves of garlic (pressed), and salt and pepper to taste. Refrigerate for at least 1 hour before serving, longer if possible. If desired, you can add fresh dill.

VEGETABLE FRITTATA

SERVES 4 ♦ ACTIVE TIME: 20 MINUTES ♦ START TO FINISH: 40 MINUTES

Make this veggie-loaded egg dish as a hearty breakfast or a light dinner. It's a perfect thing to cook up with fresh ingredients bought at the local farmer's market.

6 eggs

3 tablespoons butter

½ onion, minced

2 cloves garlic, minced

2 carrots, sliced thin

½ small zucchini, sliced thin

1 red pepper, seeded and sliced thin

⅓ cup parsley, chopped fine

Salt and pepper to taste

1 teaspoon red pepper flakes, if desired

1. Preheat the broiler to low.

2. In a bowl, whisk the eggs until combined.

3. Heat the skillet over medium-high heat. Melt the butter in the skillet. Add the onions and garlic and cook, stirring, until onions are translucent, about 3 minutes.

4. Add the carrots and zucchini slices, lower the heat to medium, and cook, stirring occasionally, until softened, about 5 minutes. Add the red pepper and continue to cook, stirring, for 2 minutes. Add the parsley.

5. Pour the eggs over the vegetables. Shake the skillet to distribute evenly. Season with salt and pepper, and sprinkle with red pepper flakes if desired. Cover and cook until eggs are set, about 10 minutes.

6. Put the skillet in the oven and cook for a few minutes to "toast" the top. Remove from the oven and let sit for a few minutes before serving.

There are so many delicious ingredients in this frittata that it's practically a one-pan meal. Make it even heartier by adding sweet potatoes. Wash a large sweet potato and pierce it all over with a fork. Put it on a paper towel in the microwave and cook for 3 minutes. Using a dish towel because it will be hot, turn the potato over and cook another 2 or 3 minutes. Allow to cool for a minute or so, and cut the potato into bite-sized pieces. Add it to the frittata after the red peppers.

SMOKED SALMON FRITTATA

SERVES 4 ✦ ACTIVE TIME: 20 MINUTES ✦ START TO FINISH: 30 MINUTES

Salmon is a high-protein, low-fat food that adds lots of flavor, texture, and—best of all— taste! Combined with the almost sweetness of leeks, this recipe is one you'll want to use for a special brunch.

2 leeks, white-part only

2 tablespoons olive oil

1 tablespoon butter

8 eggs

½ cup cream or half-and-half

1 teaspoon salt

Freshly ground black pepper

4 oz. smoked salmon, chopped

3-oz. package cream cheese, softened and cut into bits

1. Preheat the broiler to low.

2. Slice the white part of the leaks into thin slices. Put them in a colander, separating the circles. Rinse thoroughly to be sure there is no fine dirt or sand. Dry the leeks in paper towels.

3. Heat the oil with the butter in a skillet over medium-high heat. Add the leeks and cook, stirring until translucent and tender, 3 to 5 minutes. Reduce the heat to low.

4. In a bowl, whisk the eggs until well blended, and add the cream, salt, and pepper. Pour the eggs over the leeks in the skillet and increase heat to medium. Place pieces of salmon and cream cheese on top of the eggs. Cover the skillet and let cook until set, about 10 minutes. Place the skillet in the oven under the broiler to "toast" the top, about 2 minutes.

If you like dill, it makes an excellent garnish for this very tasty frittata. Finally chop some sprigs and sprinkle them over the dish when it is cool. Another tasty addition is pieces of steamed asparagus, which can be sprinkled throughout at the same time as the fish and cream cheese.

HAM, HERB & TOMATO FRITTATA

SERVES 4 ✦ ACTIVE TIME: 20 MINUTES ✦ START TO FINISH: 40 MINUTES

Smoked ham provides an earthiness to this baked egg dish, which is also loaded with fresh herbs and dotted with tomatoes.

2 tablespoons butter

½ pound thick-sliced deli ham, cut into pieces

6 eggs

¼ cup milk or heavy cream

1 teaspoon salt

Freshly ground black pepper

6 cherry tomatoes, cut in half

½ cup fresh parsley, coarsely chopped

1 teaspoon fresh thyme, minced

1. Preheat the broiler to low.

2. Heat the skillet on medium-high heat. Melt the butter in the skillet, being careful not to let it burn. Add the ham to the pan and stir, cooking until just browned, about 3 minutes.

3. Whisk the eggs in a large bowl until combined. Add the milk or cream and stir. Add the salt and pepper.

4. Pour the egg mixture into the skillet. After a couple of minutes, as the eggs begin to set, add the cherry tomato halves and sprinkle the herbs over everything. Lower the heat to medium or low, cover, and finish cooking until eggs are set, another 10 minutes. Place the skillet under the broiler for just a couple of minutes to "toast" the top.

5. Allow to sit for a few minutes. Season with additional salt and pepper, and serve.

This is one of those fritattas into which you could add almost anything tasty in the fridge. Substitute cooked chicken pieces for the ham; sprinkle leftover sautéed greens over the eggs; add some chopped jalapeños for extra flavor and heat. Have fun experimenting.

CREPES

These are very thin pancakes that can be filled with any number of things. The batter can be made with or without sugar, depending on whether you want to fill them with savory or sweet ingredients. Making them for the first time is intimidating, as it involves getting the right amount of batter on the skillet that's heated to the right temperature, but once you get the hang of it, it's a very satisfying experience that yields great results!

4 tablespoons melted butter

3 eggs

⅛ teaspoon salt

1 cup whole milk (possibly more)

1 cup flour (minus 2 tablespoons)

1. Heat the skillet over low heat to melt 2 tablespoons of the butter very slowly.

2. In a large mixing bowl, whisk the eggs until smooth. Add the salt and milk and whisk together until well blended. Whisk in the flour and, while whisking, add 2 tablespoons of the melted butter. Keep whisking until the batter is smooth and there are no lumps. Cover the bowl with plastic wrap or a clean dish towel, put in a cool, dark place, and let rest for 3 or 4 hours before making the crepes.

3. You'll need a spatula that won't scratch the surface of the skillet. Have that and a ladle for scooping out the batter ready by the stove.

4. Heat the skillet over medium-high heat and melt a slice of the remaining 2 tablespoons of butter in it. Stir the crepe batter to blend again. When the skillet is hot but not smoking (the butter should not brown), use the ladle to scoop about ¼ cup into the skillet. When the batter hits the pan, tilt it gently to spread the batter evenly over the bottom. When the bottom is covered, cook for just over 1 minute and then flip the crepe over and cook the other side for about half the time. Tilt the skillet over a plate to slide the crepe out.

5. You should be able to make several crepes per slice of butter, but gauge the pan by how dry it is, and if you think it needs butter, add some. If the pan gets too hot and the butter browns, wipe it out with a paper towel and start over.

6. Continue making the crepes until all the batter is used up. As they cool on the plate, put pieces of waxed paper between them to keep them from sticking together. If you're not going to use them right away, wrap the stack in aluminum foil and keep them in the refrigerator or freeze them.

Variations

- To make dessert crepes, add 3 tablespoons of sugar when you add the flour, and 2 tablespoons Cognac (or 1 tablespoon vanilla) once the batter is mixed.

- For dessert crepes, smother a warm crepe with chocolate-hazelnut spread sprinkled with crushed roasted, salted peanuts or cashews. You can also spread a cooled dessert crepe with cream cheese and your favorite jam. Or spread a dessert crepe with a thin layer of peanut butter and top with thinly-sliced bananas.

- Fill savory crepes with a variety of cooked meats, poultry, or fish, in a sauce. For example, you can use pieces of leftover chicken in a cream sauce with peas and mushrooms. Roll a generous spoonful up in the crepe, tuck it into a baking dish (with others), sprinkle with shredded cheese and bake in the oven at 350 degrees for about 10 minutes.

- Cook some spicy Italian sausage, spread some ricotta on the crepe, add the sausage, season with salt and pepper, roll up and put in a baking dish, cover with marinara and shredded mozzarella, and bake at 350 degrees for about 15 minutes.

CHICKEN AND MUSHROOM CREPES

**SERVES 8 TO 10 (ABOUT 16 CREPES) ✦ ACTIVE TIME: 60 MINUTES ✦
START TO FINISH: 6 HOURS**

Make this filling with leftover chicken and transform what might be a boring dinner into an elegant French dining experience.

For the Crepes

4 tablespoons melted butter

3 eggs

⅛ teaspoon salt

1 cup whole milk (possibly more)

1 cup flour (minus 2 tablespoons)

For the Filling

4 tablespoons butter

1 pound mushrooms, stems removed and cut into pieces

1 to 2 cups cooked chicken, cut into small pieces

2 tablespoons Madeira or Vermouth

1 can cream of mushroom soup

⅓ cup milk

2 tablespoons parsley, chopped

Salt and pepper to taste

1. Heat the skillet over low heat to melt 2 tablespoons of the butter very slowly.

2. In a large mixing bowl, whisk the eggs until smooth. Add the salt and milk and whisk together until well blended. Whisk in the flour and, while whisking, add 2 tablespoons of the melted butter. Keep whisking until the batter is smooth and there are no lumps. Cover the bowl with plastic wrap or a clean dish towel, put in a cool, dark place, and let rest for 3 or 4 hours before making the crepes.

3. While the crepe batter is settling, prepare the filling. Wipe down your skillet and melt the butter in it over medium heat. Add the mushroom pieces and cook, stirring frequently, until softened and lightly browned, about 5 to 8 minutes. Add the chicken pieces, Madeira or Vermouth, mushroom soup, and milk. Stir to combine and continue to cook until well blended, about 3 minutes. Stir in the chopped parsley. Add salt and pepper to taste. Put the mixture into a bowl, cover, and refrigerate until the crepes are cooked and ready to be filled.

4. When the crepe batter is ready, you'll need a spatula that won't scratch the surface of the skillet. Have that and a ladle for scooping out the batter ready by the stove.

5. Heat the skillet over medium-high heat and melt a slice of the remaining 2 tablespoons of butter in it. Stir the crepe batter to blend again. When the skillet is hot but not smoking (the butter should not brown), use the ladle to scoop about ¼ cup into the skillet. When the batter hits the pan, tilt it gently to spread the batter evenly over the bottom. When the bottom is covered, cook for just over 1 minute and then flip the crepe over and cook the other side for about half the time. Tilt the skillet over a plate to slide the crepe out.

6. You should be able to make several crepes per slice of butter, but gauge the pan by how dry it is, and if you think it needs butter, add some. If the pan gets too hot and the butter browns, wipe it out with a paper towel and start over.

7. Continue making the crepes until all the batter is used up. As they cool on the plate, put pieces of waxed paper between them to keep them from sticking together.

8. Preheat the oven to 350 degrees. Take the chicken/mushroom mixture out of the refrigerator to bring to room temperature.

9. Lightly grease a 9x13 inch baking dish. Working with one crepe at a time, put a generous scoop of the chicken mixture in the middle and fold the crepe up around the filling. Place the crepe in the baking dish so that the folded part faces down. When the baking dish is filled with the stuffed crepes, cover the dish with foil and bake for about 30 minutes until the filling is bubbling and hot.

10. Remove the foil and let cool for a few minutes before serving.

ITALIAN CREPES

SERVES 8 TO 10 (ABOUT 16 CREPES) ✦ ACTIVE TIME: 60 MINUTES ✦
START TO FINISH: 6 HOURS

I'm not sure that the French would think this is a good idea, but as far as flavor combinations go, this works. Using crepes instead of pizza dough essentially produces a less bready calzone. Mangia!

For the Crepes

4 tablespoons melted butter

3 eggs

⅛ teaspoon salt

1 cup whole milk (possibly more)

1 cup flour (minus 2 tablespoons)

For the Filling

1 pound Italian sausage, sweet, hot or a combination

4 cloves garlic, minced

1 package frozen spinach, thawed and squeezed dry

1 (15.5-oz.) can diced tomatoes, drained

Salt and Pepper to taste

8 oz. ricotta cheese

2 cups shredded mozzarella

1. Heat the skillet over low heat to melt 2 tablespoons of the butter very slowly.

2. In a large mixing bowl, whisk the eggs until smooth. Add the salt and milk and whisk together until well blended. Whisk in the flour and, while whisking, add 2 tablespoons of the melted butter. Keep whisking until the batter is smooth and there are no lumps. Cover the bowl with plastic wrap or a clean dish towel, put in a cool, dark place, and let rest for 3 or 4 hours before making the crepes.

3. While the crepe batter is settling, prepare the filling. Wipe down your skillet, over medium-high heat, cook the sausage until it's only slightly pink inside. Drain the residual fat and add the garlic. Lower the heat to medium and cook until the sausage is cooked through, stirring frequently, about 5 minutes. Add the spinach and tomatoes and stir to combine. Season with salt and pepper. Transfer to a bowl, cover and refrigerate until ready to make the crepes.

4. When the crepe batter is ready, you'll need a spatula that won't scratch the surface of the skillet. Have that and a ladle for scooping out the batter ready by the stove.

5. Heat the skillet over medium-high heat and melt a slice of the remaining 2 tablespoons of butter in it. Stir the crepe batter to blend again. When the skillet is hot but not smoking (the butter should not brown), use the ladle to scoop about ¼ cup into the skillet. When the batter hits the pan, tilt it gently to spread the batter evenly over the bottom. When the bottom is covered, cook for just over 1 minute and then flip the crepe over and cook the other side for about half the time. Tilt the skillet over a plate to slide the crepe out.

6. You should be able to make several crepes per slice of butter, but gauge the pan by how dry it is, and if you think it needs butter, add some. If the pan gets too hot and the butter browns, wipe it out with a paper towel and start over.

7. Continue making the crepes until all the batter is used up. As they cool on the plate, put pieces of waxed paper between them to keep them from sticking together.

8. Preheat the oven to 350 degrees. Take the sausage/spinach mixture out of the refrigerator and stir in the ricotta cheese. Season with additional salt and pepper if desired.

9. Lightly grease a 9x13 inch baking dish. Working with one crepe at a time, put a generous scoop of the sausage mixture in the middle and fold the crepe up around the filling. Place the crepe in the baking dish so that the folded part faces down. When the baking dish is filled with the stuffed crepes, sprinkle them with the mozzarella. Cover the dish with foil and bake for about 20 minutes until hot. Remove the foil and cook for another 5 to 10 minutes until the cheese is bubbly and just browned. Serve immediately.

BLINIS

SERVES 6 TO 8 ✦ ACTIVE TIME: 60 MINUTES ✦ START TO FINISH: 60 MINUTES

These Russian pancakes are traditionally served with sour cream and caviar. They make great "fancy" breakfast pancakes that can be served with all sorts of different toppings (see sidebar).

½ cup whole wheat flour

1 tablespoon sugar

¼ teaspoon salt

½ teaspoon baking powder

2 eggs, beaten

2½ cups milk

2 tablespoons vegetable oil

1. In a large bowl, whisk together the flour, sugar, salt, and baking powder.

2. In a smaller bowl, combine the eggs and milk, stirring to combine. Add the liquid into the dry ingredients and stir to blend thoroughly.

3. Heat a skillet over medium-high heat and brush with some of the vegetable oil. Spoon just about a tablespoon of batter to form each blini. You should be able to fit about 4 at a time in the skillet. Cook for about 2 minutes a side (or less), flipping when the edges start to crisp. These cook up fast, so be careful not to overcook them.

4. Keep the blini warm in the oven on very low heat until ready to serve.

If you like caviar of any kind, you have to try these with a dollop of sour cream or crème fraîche topped with caviar. Other great toppings include assorted jams; sour cream with a sprig of dill; scrambled eggs and hot sauce; scrambled eggs, bacon bits, and sour cream; honey-butter.

MASHED POTATO BLINIS

SERVES 6 TO 12 (ABOUT 12 PANCAKES) ✦ ACTIVE TIME: 30 MINUTES ✦ START TO FINISH: 60 MINUTES

If it ever happens that you have leftover mashed potatoes (in our house it's rare, but can happen), then this is what you need to make with them. There's something otherworldly about these. The soft, buttery-chive mashed potato inside with a crispy crust outside explodes with flavor in your mouth.

2 cups mashed potatoes

3 oz. fresh chèvre (goat cheese)

2 tablespoons finely chopped chives

2 eggs, beaten

2–3 tablespoons flour

Salt and freshly ground pepper to taste

3 tablespoons butter

1. Preheat the oven to 200 degrees.

2. In a large bowl, combine the mashed potatoes with the chèvre and chives. Add the eggs and stir. Add the flour 1 tablespoon at a time until the dough is the consistency of thick pancake batter. Season with salt and pepper.

3. Melt the butter in the skillet over medium-high heat. Make small pancakes with spoonfuls of batter, leaving room in between them. You should be able to fit 4 comfortably. Cook until browned on one side (about 2 minutes), flip and brown on the other side.

4. Place cooked pancakes on a plate, cover with foil, and put in the oven to keep warm until all are cooked and ready to serve.

Variations

You can serve these with so many toppings! Here are some favorites:

- Sour cream and caviar
- Sour cream and smoked salmon
- Smoked salmon and caviar
- Chunky applesauce
- Scrambled eggs with bacon pieces
- Fried eggs and salsa
- Sliced avocado and salsa
- Sliced avocado and smoked salmon

TORTILLAS

SERVES 6 TO 12 (ABOUT 12 LARGE TORTILLAS) ✦ **ACTIVE TIME: 30 MINUTES** ✦
START TO FINISH: 50 TO 60 MINUTES

We are covering flatbreads from around the world, so now, on to Mexico! These are even simpler to make than the ones that involved yeast. There's no need to let the dough rise for tortillas—simply mix, knead, and shape—all with your hands, which is really fun. Then cook. Oh, and eat!

3 cups flour

1 teaspoon salt

2 teaspoons baking powder

3 tablespoons Crisco shortening (or 4 tablespoons chilled butter)

1½ cups water at room temperature

1. Put the flour in a large bowl. Mix in the salt and baking powder.

2. Add the shortening (or butter), and using your fingers, blend it into the flour mix until you have a crumbly dough. Add 1 cup of the water and work it in, then portions of the additional ½ cup, working it in with your hands, so that you create a dough that's not too sticky.

3. Lightly flour a work surface and turn out the dough. Knead it for about 10 minutes until it's soft and elastic. Divide it into 12 equal pieces.

4. Using a lightly floured rolling pin, roll each piece out to almost the size of the bottom of the skillet.

5. Heat the skillet over high heat. Add a tortilla. Cook for just 15 seconds a side, flipping to cook both sides. Keep the cooked tortillas warm by putting them on a plate covered with a damp tea towel. Serve warm.

A homemade tortilla begs for a filling of sliced, grilled meat with shredded cheese, chopped tomatoes, chopped red onions, chopped lettuce, and sliced jalapeños.

YORKSHIRE PUDDING

SERVES 4 TO 6 ✦ ACTIVE TIME: 30 MINUTES ✦ START TO FINISH: 60 MINUTES

*This incredible treat is like a savory Dutch baby—a large (and so delicious!) popover.
It's traditionally served with roast beef and is, in fact, made with the juices from the meat.
Begin your preparation about an hour before the meat will be ready, as the batter needs
to sit for a while. My mouth waters just thinking about this classic combination.*

1½ cups flour

¾ teaspoon salt

¾ cup milk, room
temperature

3 large eggs, room
temperature

¾ cup water, room
temperature

½ cup beef drippings

1. Preheat the oven to 400 degrees or increase the temperature when you take
   your roast beef out of the oven.

2. In a large bowl, mix the flour and salt together with a whisk. Make a well
   in the center of the flour, add the milk and whisk until blended. Next beat
   the eggs into the batter until thoroughly combined. Add the water, stir this
   in thoroughly, and set aside for about an hour.

3. When your roast comes out of the oven, pour off ½ cup of drippings
   and put them in the skillet. Put the skillet in the oven and let the drippings
   get very hot so that they sizzle. Stir the batter while you're waiting so it's
   blended. Remove the skillet from the oven, pour the batter in, and return
   it immediately.

4. Bake for about 30 minutes or until the sides have risen and are gently browned.

5. Bring to the table where the roast beef awaits, and serve with extra juices
   on the side.

If you want to make this delicious side dish but you're not having
roast beef, you can substitute 1/2 cup melted butter for the drippings.
Their smoking point is lower than the drippings, so keep an eye
on the skillet as it heats up in the oven. The butter will be sizzling
before long.

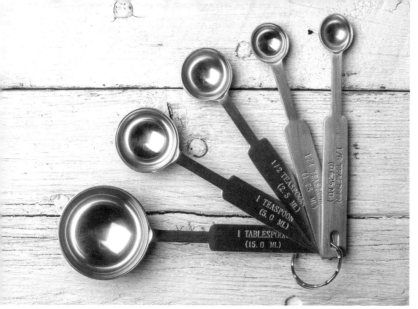

CAKES
& PIES

If you've never baked a cake or pie in a cast-iron skillet before, you are probably wondering whether it's even worth it. After all, specialized cookware was developed specifically for these kinds of desserts, right? The standard 8-inch round cake pan, and the quintessential tapered and trimmed pie plate—these are what you make cakes and pies in. Until now. I can assure you that not only is it often easier to make cakes and pies in the cast-iron skillet, but also the flavor results are often superior. You won't be turning out cakes that need to be stacked and frosted (all the better!), or pies that have an extra frill of crust around the edge, but you will be producing treats that you and your family and friends will love. I know, because these disappeared soon after they were made.

NUTTY APPLE–CRANBERRY PIE

SERVES 6 TO 8 ◆ ACTIVE TIME: 60 MINUTES ◆ START TO FINISH: 2 HOURS

If you and your family like something a bit sweet-tart, you'll love this pie. The sweetness of the apples pairs wonderfully with the tartness of fresh cranberries, and the toasted walnuts add a buttery earthiness.

1 cup chopped walnuts

4 pounds Granny Smith apples

1 cup fresh cranberries

1 teaspoon ground cinnamon

¼ teaspoon ground ginger

1 cup sugar

1 teaspoon lemon juice

8 tablespoons (1 stick) butter

1 cup light brown sugar

1 pre-made refrigerator pie dough (14.1 oz) or homemade pie dough (page 146)

1 egg white

2 tablespoons sugar

1. Preheat the oven to 450 degrees.

2. Spread the walnut pieces out on a cookie sheet and bake until toasted, about 5 to 8 minutes, removing the cookie sheet mid-way to shake and turn the nuts. Keep an eye on them so they don't burn. Remove the cookie sheet from the oven and allow the nuts to cool. Reduce the oven temperature to 350 degrees.

3. Peel and core the apples, and cut into ½-inch-thick wedges. In a large bowl, combine the apples with cranberries, cinnamon, ginger, sugar, and lemon juice. Stir in the walnut pieces.

4. Put the skillet over medium heat and melt the butter in it. Add the brown sugar and cook, stirring constantly, until sugar is dissolved, one or two minutes. Remove pan from heat.

5. Roll out 1 of the piecrusts and gently place it over the sugar mixture. Fill with the apple/cranberry mix, and place the other crust over the apples, crimping the edges together.

6. Brush the top crust with the egg white, and sprinkle the sugar over it. Cut 4 or 5 slits in the middle.

7. Put the skillet in the oven and bake for 60 to 70 minutes until golden brown and bubbly. Cover the outermost edge with aluminum foil in the last 10 minutes of baking to prevent it from burning.

8. Allow to cool before serving.

PALEO PIE CRUST

You can make any pie a "Paleo pie" with a few key ingredient swaps, starting with the perfect Paleo crust! This recipe makes a delicious Paleo-friendly pie crust (single crust).

½ cup each rice, tapioca, and potato starch flours

¼ cup potato starch flour

2 teaspoons xanthan gum

½ teaspoon salt

Dash of sugar

4 tablespoons lard, ghee, or coconut oil

4 or 5 tablespoons very cold water

1. Combine the flours, xanthan gum, salt, and sugar. Work the fat into the flour.

2. When a crumbly dough forms, add the water 2 tablespoons at a time, working it with your fingers until it holds together.

3. Transfer to a lightly floured surface and form a patty. Wrap in plastic and refrigerate about 1 hour before rolling.

PEACH PIE

SERVES 6 TO 8 ✦ ACTIVE TIME: 60 MINUTES ✦ START TO FINISH: 2 HOURS

There's something otherworldly about a pie made with fresh peaches. It is just so good! With the way the cast-iron skillet yields a sugary, somewhat crunchy bottom crust, this will become your go-to recipe when peaches are in season.

2–3 pounds peaches to yield 4 cups peeled and sliced

1 tablespoon lemon juice

¾ cup sugar

4 tablespoons flour

8 tablespoons (1 stick) butter

1 cup light brown sugar

1 pre-made refrigerator pie dough (14.1 oz) or homemade pie dough (page 146)

1 egg white

2 tablespoons sugar

1. Preheat the oven to 350 degrees.

2. Bring a large pot of water to boil. Fill another large pot with cold water. When the water's boiling, submerge the peaches for a minute or two, then remove them with a slotted spoon and put them immediately into the cold water. This loosens the skin and makes them much easier to peel. Use enough peaches to yield 4 cups of peeled slices. Put the slices in a bowl and add the lemon juice, sugar, and flour. Stir to combine.

3. Put the skillet over medium heat and melt the butter in it. Add the brown sugar and cook, stirring constantly, until sugar is dissolved, one or two minutes. Remove pan from heat.

4. Roll out 1 of the piecrusts and gently place it over the sugar mixture. Fill with the peaches, and place the other crust over the peaches, crimping the edges together.

5. Brush the top crust with the egg white, and sprinkle the sugar over it. Cut 4 or 5 slits in the middle.

6. Put the skillet in the oven and bake for 60 to 70 minutes until golden brown and bubbly. Cover the outermost edge with aluminum foil in the last 10 minutes of baking to prevent it from burning.

7. Allow to cool before serving. Serve with bourbon whipped cream.

For this pie you have to try serving it with bourbon whipped cream. You'll understand why this is so popular in the south, from whence the best peaches—and bourbon—hail. Simply beat heavy or whipping cream until soft peaks form. Add about 1/4 cup sugar and continue beating until stiff peaks form. Gently beat in 1/4 cup bourbon.

BLUEBERRY PIE

SERVES 6 TO 8 ✦ ACTIVE TIME: 60 MINUTES ✦ START TO FINISH: 2 HOURS

Blueberry pie is so easy to make and tastes so good with rich, creamy vanilla ice cream. Summer in a slice!

4 cups fresh or frozen blueberries

1 tablespoon lemon juice

1 cup sugar

3 tablespoons flour

8 tablespoons (1 stick) butter

1 cup light brown sugar

1 pre-made refrigerator pie dough (14.1 oz) or homemade pie dough (page 146)

1 egg white

2 tablespoons sugar

1. Preheat the oven to 350 degrees.

2. If using frozen blueberries, it's not necessary to thaw them completely. Put the blueberries in a large bowl, add the lemon juice, sugar, and flour. Stir to combine.

3. Put the skillet over medium heat and melt the butter in it. Add the brown sugar and cook, stirring constantly, until sugar is dissolved, one or two minutes. Remove pan from heat.

4. Roll out 1 of the piecrusts and gently place it over the sugar mixture. Fill with the blueberries, and place the other crust over the blueberries, crimping the edges together.

5. Brush the top crust with the egg white, and sprinkle the sugar over it. Cut 4 or 5 slits in the middle.

6. Put the skillet in the oven and bake for 50 to 60 minutes until golden brown and bubbly. Cover the outermost edge with aluminum foil in the last 10 minutes of baking to prevent it from burning.

7. Allow to cool before serving.

VERY CHERRY PIE

SERVES 6 TO 8 ◆ **ACTIVE TIME: 60 MINUTES** ◆ **START TO FINISH: 2 HOURS**

What I love about making this pie is working with the cherries. It takes time to slice and pit them, and I use this time to whet my appetite for the final result by eating cherries as I work. A few for the pie, a few for me…the simple things! I also prefer to only use fresh cherries for pie, as there is no substitute for the flavor. Use one variety or a combination.

4 cups fresh cherries, pitted

1 tablespoon lemon juice

1 cup sugar

1½ tablespoons flour

8 tablespoons (1 stick) butter

1 cup light brown sugar

1 pre-made refrigerator pie dough (14.1 oz) or homemade pie dough (page 146)

1 egg white

2 tablespoons sugar

1. Preheat the oven to 350 degrees.

2. Pitting the cherries takes time, but it's worth it. Work with clean cherries and put a piece of waxed paper over the area where you'll be working, as the juice will drip and stain. Have your measuring cup ready to put the cherries in when they're pitted.

3. Use toothpicks or tweezers with a pointed end or the kind of tool to get lobster meat out of the shell—something small and sharp on the end. Remove the stem from the cherry, insert the toothpick or tool next to the pit, and circle the pit until it can be scooped out.

4. When you have 4 cups of pitted cherries, put them in a large bowl, add the lemon juice, sugar, and flour. Stir to combine.

5. Put the skillet over medium heat and melt the butter in it. Add the brown sugar and cook, stirring constantly, until sugar is dissolved, one or two minutes. Remove pan from heat.

6. Roll out 1 of the piecrusts and gently place it over the sugar mixture. Fill with the cherries, and place the other crust over the cherries, crimping the edges together.

7. Brush the top crust with the egg white, and sprinkle the sugar over it. Cut 4 or 5 slits in the middle.

8. Put the skillet in the oven and bake for 50 to 60 minutes until golden brown and bubbly. Cover the outermost edge with aluminum foil in the last 10 minutes of baking to prevent it from burning.

9. Allow to cool before serving.

APPLE PIE

SERVES 6 TO 8 ✦ ACTIVE TIME: 60 MINUTES ✦ START TO FINISH: 2 HOURS

Impress your friends! Impress your family! Impress yourself—you won't believe how easy this is and how delicious the result!

4 pounds Granny Smith apples

1 teaspoon ground cinnamon

¾ cup sugar

1 teaspoon lemon juice

8 tablespoons (1 stick) butter

1 cup light brown sugar

1 pre-made refrigerator pie dough (14.1 oz) or homemade pie dough (page 146)

1 egg white

2 tablespoons sugar

1. Preheat the oven to 350 degrees.

2. Peel and core the apples, and cut into ½-inch-thick wedges. Toss apples with cinnamon, sugar, and lemon juice.

3. Put the skillet over medium heat and melt the butter in it. Add the brown sugar and cook, stirring constantly, until sugar is dissolved, one or two minutes. Remove pan from heat.

4. Roll out 1 of the piecrusts and gently place it over the sugar mixture. Fill with the apple/spice mix, and place the other crust over the apples, crimping the edges together.

5. Brush the top crust with the egg white, and sprinkle the sugar over it. Cut 4 or 5 slits in the middle.

6. Put the skillet in the oven and bake for 60 to 70 minutes until golden brown and bubbly. Cover the outermost edge with aluminum foil in the last 10 minutes of baking to prevent it from burning.

7. Allow to cool before serving. Serve with whipped cream or ice cream.

You can flavor whipped cream with liqueur for an especially yummy topping. Beat heavy or whipping cream until soft peaks form. Add about 1/4 cup sugar and continue beating until stiff peaks form. Gently beat in 1/4 cup liqueur, such as apple brandy or Cointreau.

GRAPE PIE

SERVES 6 TO 8 ✦ ACTIVE TIME: 60 MINUTES ✦ START TO FINISH: 90 MINUTES

A refreshing twist on tarte tatin, though it's a similar concept: fruit embedded in pastry cream. Sliced grapes make a beautiful presentation, and the taste is just as nice. Serve with a white dessert wine, like an Ice Wine.

2–3 cups seedless grapes, sliced in half (white, red or a combination)

1 (10-oz.) jar lemon curd

1 tablespoon lemon juice

1 teaspoon lemon zest

8 tablespoons (1 stick) butter

1 cup light brown sugar

1 pre-made refrigerator pie dough (14.1 oz) or homemade pie dough (page 146)

2 tablespoons sugar

1. Preheat the oven to 350 degrees.

2. In a small bowl, combine the lemon curd, lemon juice, and lemon zest. Set aside.

3. Put the skillet over medium heat and melt the butter in it. Add the brown sugar and cook, stirring constantly, until sugar is dissolved, one or two minutes. Remove pan from heat.

4. Roll out 1 of the piecrusts and gently place it over the sugar mixture. Remove the skillet from the heat.

5. Spread the lemon curd over the piecrust. Place the grape halves in a decorative pattern on top of the lemon curd, skin side up. Sprinkle with sugar.

6. Put the skillet in the oven and bake for 45 to 50 minutes until set. Allow to cool before serving.

Variations

For some added crunch and a bit of complementary saltiness, sprinkle the pie with roasted, salted pumpkin seeds. Their lovely green color complements the grapes, too.

PUMPKIN PIE

SERVES 6 TO 8 ✦ ACTIVE TIME: 30 MINUTES ✦ START TO FINISH: 90 MINUTES

With the butter/sugar combo underneath the pie shell, the result is a crisp, sweet crust topped with an earthy, smooth pumpkin filling. It really works.

1 (15-oz.) can pumpkin purée

1 (12-oz.) can evaporated milk

2 eggs, lightly beaten

½ cup sugar

½ teaspoon salt

1 teaspoon cinnamon

¼ teaspoon ground ginger

¼ teaspoon ground nutmeg

8 tablespoons (1 stick) butter

1 cup light brown sugar

1 pre-made refrigerator pie dough (14.1 oz) or homemade pie dough (page 146)

1. Preheat the oven to 400 degrees.

2. In a large bowl, combine the pumpkin purée, evaporated milk, eggs, sugar, salt, cinnamon, ginger, and nutmeg. Stir to combine thoroughly.

3. Put the skillet over medium heat and melt the butter in it. Add the brown sugar and cook, stirring constantly, until sugar is dissolved, one or two minutes. Remove pan from heat.

4. Roll out 1 of the piecrusts and gently place it over the sugar mixture. Fill with the pumpkin mix.

5. Put the skillet in the oven and bake for 15 minutes, then reduce the heat to 325 degrees and bake an additional 30 to 45 minutes until the filling is firm and a toothpick inserted in the middle comes out clean. Don't overcook.

6. Remove from the oven and allow to cool before serving. Serve with fresh whipped cream laced with a splash of apple liquor like Calvados or Applejack.

Paleo Variation

To convert this classic pie to a paleo dessert, simply substitute a Paleo Pie Crust for the flour-based crust (see page 183 for the recipe) and substitute ¾ cup coconut milk for the evaporated milk. Don't cook the brown sugar in the butter to prep the skillet. Instead, melt some coconut oil to lightly grease the skillet before putting the crust on it.

FRENCH APPLE TART

SERVES 6 TO 8 ✦ ACTIVE TIME: 60 MINUTES ✦ START TO FINISH: 90 MINUTES

This is the quintessential example of how the cast-iron skillet caramelizes fruits to perfection. It's what the French call "tarte tatin," and for them it's a national treasure.

1 cup flour

½ teaspoon salt

1 tablespoon sugar

6 tablespoons unsalted butter, cut into small pieces

3 tablespoons ice water

1 cup (2 sticks) unsalted butter, cut into small pieces

1½ cups sugar

8 to 10 apples, peeled, cored, and halved (see sidebar)

The best apples for this dessert are ones that are semi-tart and crisp. These include Mutsu, Honeycrisp, Jonagold, and Golden Delicious.

1. To make the pastry, whisk together the flour, salt, and sugar in a large bowl. Using your fingers, work the butter into the flour mixture until you have coarse clumps. Sprinkle the ice water over the mixture and continue to work it with your hands until it just holds together. Shape it into a ball, wrap it in plastic wrap, and refrigerate it for at least one hour, or even overnight.

2. Place the pieces of butter evenly over the bottom of the skillet, then sprinkle the sugar evenly over everything. Next, start placing the apple halves in a circular pattern, starting on the outside of the pan and working in. The halves should support each other and all face the same direction. Place either one or two halves in the center when finished working around the outside. As the cake bakes, the slices will slide down a bit.

3. Place the skillet on the oven and turn the heat to medium-high. Cook the apples in the pan, uncovered, until the sugar and butter start to caramelize, about 35 minutes. While they're cooking, spoon some of the melted juices over the apples (but don't overdo it).

4. Preheat the oven to 400 degrees, and position a rack in the center.

5. Take the chilled dough out of the refrigerator and, working on a lightly floured surface, roll it out into a circle just big enough to cover the skillet (about 12 to 14 inches). Gently drape the pastry over the apples, tucking the pastry in around the sides.

6. Put the skillet in the oven and bake for about 25 minutes, until the pastry is golden brown.

7. Remove the skillet from the oven and allow to cool for about 5 minutes. Find a plate that is an inch or two larger than the top of the skillet and place it over the top. You will be inverting the tart onto the plate. Be sure to use oven mitts or secure pot holders, as the skillet will be hot.

8. Holding the plate tightly against the top of the skillet, turn the skillet over so the plate is now on the bottom. If some of the apples are stuck to the bottom, gently remove them and place them on the tart.

9. Allow to cool a few more minutes, or set aside until ready to serve (it's better if it's served warm).

10. Serve with fresh whipped cream, crème fraiche, or vanilla ice cream.

PINEAPPLE UPSIDE-DOWN CAKE

SERVES 8 TO 10 ✦ ACTIVE TIME: 60 MINUTES ✦ START TO FINISH: 2 HOURS

This is another recipe that is cooked to perfection in cast-iron. You'll see!

Fruit

4 tablespoons butter

1 (18-oz.) can pineapple rings, plus juice

½ cup dark brown sugar

Maraschino cherries (optional)

Cake

4 tablespoons butter, chilled

1 cup light brown sugar

2 eggs

1 cup buttermilk

1 teaspoon vanilla extract

1½ cups flour

1½ teaspoons baking powder

½ teaspoon salt

1. Preheat the oven to 350 degrees.

2. Heat the skillet over medium-high heat. Add the butter, and stir in the juice from the jar of pineapples and the brown sugar. Stir continuously while the sugar melts, and continue stirring until the liquid boils and starts to thicken. Cook until the sauce turns a thick, dark, caramel consistency.

3. Remove from heat and place the pineapple rings in the liquid, working from the outside in. Place a cherry in each ring if adding cherries. Put the skillet in the oven while preparing the batter.

4. To make the cake, beat the cold butter and light brown sugar with an electric mixer until light and creamy. Beat in the eggs one at a time, making sure the first is thoroughly mixed in before adding the next.

5. In a small bowl, whisk together the flour, baking powder, and salt. In another small bowl, stir the buttermilk and vanilla together. Alternate adding the dry and liquid ingredients to the butter/sugar mix until all are combined but not overly smooth.

6. Remove the skillet from the oven and pour the batter over the pineapple rings. Replace in the oven and bake for 45 minutes until cake is golden and a knife inserted in the middle comes out clean.

7. Take the skillet out of the oven and let it rest for about 10 minutes.

8. Find a plate that is an inch or two larger than the top of the skillet and place it over the top. You will be inverting the cake onto the plate. Be sure to use oven mitts or secure pot holders, as the skillet will be hot. Holding the plate tightly against the top of the skillet, turn the skillet over so the plate is now on the bottom. If some of the pineapple is stuck to the bottom, gently remove it and place it on the cake.

9. Allow to cool a few more minutes, or set aside until ready to serve (it's better if it's served warm).

In 1925, Dole sponsored a pineapple recipe contest, promising to publish winning recipes in a book. It received over 50,000 recipes, and over 2,000 of them were for pineapple upside-down cake. It's been a classic of American cooking ever since.

BLUEBERRY UPSIDE-DOWN CAKE

SERVES 8 TO 10 ✦ ACTIVE TIME: 60 MINUTES ✦ START TO FINISH: 2 HOURS

This twist on the traditional pineapple upside-down cake, and it's equally elegant and delicious.

Fruit

4 tablespoons butter

1½ cups fresh blueberries

½ cup dark brown sugar

2 tablespoons fresh-squeezed lemon juice

Cake

4 tablespoons butter, chilled

1 cup light brown sugar

2 eggs

1⅓ cups flour

1½ teaspoons baking powder

½ teaspoon salt

½ cup sour cream

¼ cup milk

1 teaspoon vanilla extract

1. Preheat the oven to 350 degrees.

2. Heat the skillet over medium-high heat. Add the butter. In a small bowl, gently combine the blueberries, brown sugar, and lemon juice. When the butter is melted and just bubbling, put the blueberry-sugar mix in the skillet and press the berries down into the pan. Put the skillet in the oven while preparing the batter.

3. To make the cake, beat the cold butter and light brown sugar with an electric mixer until light and creamy. Beat in the eggs one at a time, making sure the first is thoroughly mixed in before adding the next.

4. In a small bowl, whisk together the flour, baking powder, and salt. In a large measuring cup, mix the sour cream, milk, and vanilla. Alternate adding the dry and liquid ingredients to the butter/sugar mix until all are combined but not overly smooth.

5. Remove the skillet from the oven and pour the batter over the blueberries. Replace in the oven and bake for 25 minutes until cake is golden and a knife inserted in the middle comes out clean. Take the skillet out of the oven and let it rest for about 5 minutes.

6. Find a plate that is an inch or two larger than the top of the skillet and place it over the top. You will be inverting the cake onto the plate. Be sure to use oven mitts or secure pot holders, as the skillet will be hot. Holding the plate tightly against the top of the skillet, turn the skillet over so the plate is now on the bottom. If some of it is stuck to the bottom, gently remove it and place it on the cake.

7. Allow to cool a few more minutes, or set aside until ready to serve (it's better if it's served warm).

Variation

A nice sweet-tart combination is blueberries and fresh cranberries. Use 1 cup blueberries and ½ cup fresh cranberries (picked over).

RASPBERRY CORN CAKE

SERVES 4 TO 6 ✦ ACTIVE TIME: 40 MINUTES ✦ START TO FINISH: 60 MINUTES

The polenta in this cake gives it great texture, and makes it tastier, too. It also gives the cake a lovely yellow color that highlights the raspberries.

½ cup flour

½ cup finely ground polenta

½ teaspoon baking powder

¼ teaspoon baking soda

¼ teaspoon salt

½ cup milk

¼ cup maple syrup

4 tablespoons butter, cut into pieces

½ cup fresh raspberries

1. Preheat the oven to 350 degrees. Put the skillet in the oven to get it hot.

2. In a bowl, mix the flour, polenta, baking powder, baking soda, and salt. In another bowl, whisk together the milk and syrup. Stir the wet ingredients into the dry ingredients and combine thoroughly but not overly.

3. Using oven mitts or potholders, remove the hot skillet from the oven and add the pieces of butter. Pour the batter over the butter, and sprinkle the raspberries on top.

4. Put the skillet back in the oven and bake for about 20 minutes, until just set and golden, and a toothpick inserted in the middle comes out clean. Serve with vanilla ice cream and additional berries.

Variations:

- Substitute fresh blueberries, black berries, or even strawberries for the raspberries.

- For added texture and crunch, sprinkle some polenta over the top of the cake before putting it back in the oven.

- Add ¼ cup dried organic coconut and an additional ¼ cup of milk.

- Substitute unsweetened almond milk for the regular milk.

- Substitute vanilla almond milk for the milk, adding ¼ cup more and deleting the maple syrup (vanilla almond milk is sweet).

NEW ENGLAND SPIDER CAKE

SERVES 4 TO 6 ✦ ACTIVE TIME: 30 MINUTES ✦ START TO FINISH: 40 MINUTES

Early settlers in New England used a version of today's cast-iron skillet that had legs on it so it could sit in the fire. While it's essentially a recipe for cornbread, made and cooked this way the outside becomes crisp and the inside forms a custardy layer.

1¼ cups yellow corn meal

½ cup sugar

1 teaspoon baking soda

1 teaspoon salt

2 cups buttermilk

2 large eggs

2 tablespoons unsalted butter

1. Preheat the oven to 400 degrees and position a rack in the middle.

2. In a large bowl, combine the corn meal, sugar, baking soda, and salt. In a separate bowl, beat the eggs with the buttermilk until thoroughly combined. Gradually add it to the cornmeal mixture.

3. Heat the skillet over high heat and add the butter. When melted and swirled around to cover the whole bottom, pour in the batter.

4. Transfer the skillet to the oven and bake about 20 minutes, until the cake is golden brown and springy to the touch. Melt some additional butter on the surface when you take it out of the oven, and serve with jam, fresh berries, or maple syrup.

ORANGE CAKE

SERVES 6 TO 8 ✦ ACTIVE TIME: 40 ✦ START TO FINISH: 90 MINUTES

When all your friends have flown south for the winter and you're listening to a forecast for snow, stop everything and make this cake. As it's cooling, take a fragrant bubble bath, then wrap yourself in a fluffy robe, put on warm slippers, and have a piece of this cake with a glass of champagne. No sand in your swimsuit!

¾ cup sugar

Zest of two oranges (about 2 tablespoons)

8 tablespoons (1 stick) butter, cut in pieces

3 eggs

1½ cups flour

1 teaspoon baking powder

½ cup orange juice (preferably fresh-squeezed)

1. Preheat the oven to 350 degrees. Put the skillet in the oven to get it hot.

2. In a large bowl, combine the sugar and orange zest, working them together so the zest penetrates the sugar. Add the butter, and cream the butter and lemon-sugar together until light. Add the eggs one at a time, combining thoroughly after each addition.

3. In the measuring cup you use for the flour, add the baking powder and mix the dry ingredients together. Alternately add the flour mix and the orange juice to the butter-sugar mix until thoroughly combined.

4. Remove the skillet from the oven using pot holders or oven mitts. Pour the cake batter into it.

5. Put in the oven and bake for about 30 to 35 minutes, until the top is golden and the cake springs to the touch and a toothpick inserted in the middle comes out clean. Cool and cut into wedges.

6. Serve with fresh whipped cream laced with Grand Marnier liqueur and a glass of champagne.

LEMON CAKE

SERVES 6 TO 8 ✦ ACTIVE TIME: 40 MINUTES ✦ START TO FINISH: 90 MINUTES

Fragrant, moist, and bursting with the flavor of fresh lemons, this is a delightful dessert or snack.

¾ cup sugar

Zest of two lemons (about 1 tablespoon)

6 tablespoons butter, cut in pieces

2 eggs

1 cup flour

1 teaspoon baking powder

½ cup milk

1. Preheat the oven to 350 degrees.

2. In a large bowl, combine the sugar and lemon zest, working them together so the zest penetrates the sugar. Add the butter, and cream the butter and lemon-sugar together until light. Add the eggs one at a time, combining thoroughly after each addition.

3. In the measuring cup you use for the flour, add the baking powder and mix the dry ingredients together. Alternately add the flour mix and the milk to the butter-sugar mix until thoroughly combined.

4. Grease the skillet with some butter and add the cake batter.

5. Put in the oven and bake for about 30 to 35 minutes, until the top is golden and the cake springs to the touch and a toothpick inserted in the middle comes out clean. Cool and cut into wedges.

Variations

This cake is delicious on its own, but it can be topped with all kinds of treats. Consider these:

❀ Fresh-squeezed lemon juice and granulated sugar

❀ Whipped cream

❀ Fresh fruit like raspberries, strawberries, blueberries, blackberries, or a combination of berries

❀ Ice cream (almost any flavor)

❀ Pecans sautéed in butter and brown sugar

LEMON RASPBERRY CAKE

SERVES 6 TO 8 ◆ **ACTIVE TIME: 40 MINUTES** ◆ **START TO FINISH: 90 MINUTES**

Bright, beautiful, and as delicious to eat as it is to look at, this is a cake you'll find yourself making repeatedly in the summer. Serve it with fresh raspberries, blueberries, or blackberries and a dollop of whipped cream laced with framboise *liqueur.*

½ cup fresh raspberries (substitute frozen if you don't have fresh, but drain them)

1 cup + 1 tablespoon sugar

Zest of two lemons (about 1 tablespoon)

6 tablespoons butter, cut in pieces

2 eggs

1 cup flour

1 teaspoon baking powder

½ cup sour cream

1. Preheat the oven to 350 degrees. Put the skillet in the oven to get it hot.

2. In a small bowl, gently mash the raspberries and sprinkle with 1 tablespoon of sugar. Set aside.

3. In a large bowl, combine the sugar and lemon zest, working them together so the zest penetrates the sugar. Add the butter, and cream the butter and lemon-sugar together until light. Add the eggs one at a time, combining thoroughly after each addition.

4. In the measuring cup you use for the flour, add the baking powder and mix the dry ingredients together. Alternately add the flour mix and the sour cream to the butter-sugar mix until thoroughly combined. Gently stir in the mashed raspberries. Don't over mix.

5. Remove the skillet from the oven with pot holders or oven mitts, and fill with the cake batter.

6. Put in the oven and bake for about 30 to 35 minutes, until the top is golden and the cake springs to the touch and a toothpick inserted in the middle comes out clean. Cool and cut into wedges.

CHOCOLATE MALTED CAKE

SERVES 8 ◆ ACTIVE TIME: 20 MINUTES ◆ START TO FINISH: 60 MINUTES

For fans of malted milk balls and malted chocolate shakes, here's a way to sass up your chocolate cake recipe so that this rich flavor permeates it. What the heck—make an Ovaltine milk shake with vanilla ice cream to go along with it.

4 tablespoons butter

1 (15.25-oz.) box of chocolate cake mix

2 tablespoons cocoa powder

⅓ cup Rich Chocolate Ovaltine

1½ cups water

½ cup vegetable oil

6 oz. unsweetened applesauce

4 eggs

1. Preheat the oven to 350 degrees.

2. In the skillet, melt the butter over low heat.

3. In a large bowl, combine the cake mix, cocoa powder, Ovaltine, water, oil, applesauce, and eggs. Stir to combine well.

4. When the butter in the skillet is bubbling, turn off the heat and pour the batter into it.

5. Bake for 35 minutes until lightly browned on the top and sides and a toothpick inserted in the middle comes out clean.

6. Allow to cool for about 10 minutes. The skillet will still be hot. Put a large serving plate on the counter and, working quickly and deliberately, flip the skillet so the cake is inverted onto the plate.

7. Allow to cool slightly before serving.

CHOCOLATE CAKE

SERVES 4 ✦ ACTIVE TIME: 20 MINUTES ✦ START TO FINISH: 60 MINUTES

This is another winner that you'll want to serve again and again either plain or with a topping of your choice.

6 tablespoons butter, cut in pieces

1 cup sugar

2 eggs

½ teaspoon vanilla extract

1 cup flour

1 teaspoon baking powder

2 tablespoons unsweetened cocoa powder

½ cup milk

1. Preheat the oven to 350 degrees.

2. In a large bowl, cream the butter and sugar together until light. Add the eggs one at a time, combining thoroughly after each addition. Stir in the vanilla extract.

3. In a small bowl, combine the flour, baking powder, and cocoa powder, and mix the dry ingredients together. Alternately add the flour mix and the milk to the butter-sugar mix until thoroughly combined.

4. Grease the skillet with some butter and add the cake batter.

5. Put in the oven and bake for about 30 to 35 minutes, until the top is golden and the cake springs to the touch and a toothpick inserted in the middle comes out clean. Cool and cut into wedges.

Variation

There are so many ways to top this simple chocolate cake, including whipped cream, frosting, fresh berries, berries and cream, chocolate syrup, ice cream (almost any flavor), or marshmallow fluff.

CHOCOLATE MINT CAKE

SERVES 8 ✦ ACTIVE TIME: 20 MINUTES ✦ START TO FINISH: 60 MINUTES

Using Andes Thin Mints like chocolate chips gives extra flavor and texture to an already killer chocolate cake—that's so easy to make!

4 tablespoons butter

1 (15.25-oz.) box of chocolate cake mix

2 tablespoons cocoa powder

1¼ cups water

½ cup vegetable oil

6 oz. unsweetened applesauce

4 eggs

1 box of 28 Andes Thin Mints, broken into pieces

1. Preheat the oven to 350 degrees.

2. In the skillet, melt the butter over low heat.

3. In a large bowl, combine the cake mix, cocoa powder, water, oil, applesauce, and eggs. Stir to combine well. Add the Andes Thin Mints and stir until evenly distributed.

4. When the butter in the skillet is bubbling, turn off the heat and pour the batter into it.

5. Bake for 35 minutes until lightly browned on the top and sides and a toothpick inserted in the middle comes out clean.

6. Allow to cool for about 10 minutes. The skillet will still be hot. Put a large serving plate on the counter and, working quickly and deliberately, flip the skillet so the cake is inverted onto the plate.

7. Allow to cool slightly before serving, and add a scoop of mint chocolate chip ice cream for an over-the-top experience.

DOUBLE CHOCOLATE DECADENCE CAKE

SERVES 8 ✦ ACTIVE TIME: 20 MINUTES ✦ START TO FINISH: 60 MINUTES

When you are in the mood for a fudgy, easy chocolate cake, look no further than this recipe. It's so easy to make and so good. Beware!

6 tablespoons butter

1 cup semi-sweet chocolate morsels

1 (15.25-oz.) box of chocolate cake mix

1 cup water

½ cup vegetable oil

6 oz. unsweetened applesauce

4 eggs

1. Preheat the oven to 350 degrees.

2. In the skillet, melt the butter over medium heat. When it's melted, add the chocolate morsels. Melt the morsels in the butter over low to medium heat.

3. In a large bowl, combine the cake mix, water, oil, applesauce, and eggs. Stir to combine.

4. When the chocolate/butter combo is melted and hot, but not bubbling, turn off the heat and pour the batter over the chocolate.

5. Bake 35 to 40 minutes until browned on the top and sides and a toothpick inserted in the middle comes out clean.

6. Allow to cool for about 10 minutes. The skillet will still be hot. Put a large serving plate on the counter and, working quickly and deliberately, flip the skillet so the cake is inverted onto the plate.

7. Allow to cool slightly before serving.

BASIC CARROT CAKE

SERVES 8 ✦ ACTIVE TIME: 20 MINUTES ✦ START TO FINISH: 60 MINUTES

This recipe makes a delicious and moist carrot cake. It's especially tasty when frosted with an easy-to-make cream cheese frosting (see sidebar).

8 tablespoons (1 stick) butter

1 cup julienned carrots, chopped fine

1½ cups golden raisins

1 (15.25-oz.) box of carrot cake mix

¾ cup water

⅔ cup vegetable oil

6 oz. unsweetened applesauce

4 eggs

1. Preheat the oven to 350 degrees.

2. In the skillet, melt the butter over medium heat. When it's melted, add the carrots and raisins. Simmer them in the butter over low to medium heat until the butter is bubbling.

3. In a large bowl, combine the cake mix, water, oil, applesauce, and eggs. Stir to combine.

4. When the butter in the skillet is bubbling, turn off the heat and pour the batter over the carrot/raisin mix.

5. Bake 35 to 40 minutes until browned on the top and sides and a toothpick inserted in the middle comes out clean.

6. Allow to cool for about 10 minutes. The skillet will still be hot. Put a large serving plate on the counter and, working quickly and deliberately, flip the skillet so the cake is inverted onto the plate. Allow to cool before frosting.

EASY CREAM CHEESE FROSTING

This makes enough to frost the skillet cake, which is a single layer.

6 oz. cream cheese, at room temperature

4 tablespoons unsalted butter, at room temperature

1¼ cups confectioner's sugar

½ teaspoon vanilla extract

1. In a large bowl, combine all ingredients. With an electric mixer, beat on medium until well combined and smooth. Spread over cooled cake.

COSMIC CARROT CAKE

SERVES 8 ✦ ACTIVE TIME: 20 MINUTES ✦ START TO FINISH: 60 MINUTES

This recipe throws in all the goodies that make carrot cake so moist and flavorful—carrots (yes!), coconut, and pineapple. One bite and you'll know why it's nicknamed "cosmic."

8 tablespoons (1 stick) butter

1 cup julienned carrots, chopped fine

1 cup fresh chopped pineapple chunks (if using canned, drain juice)

1 (15.25-oz.) box of carrot cake mix

¾ cup water

⅔ cup vegetable oil

6 oz. unsweetened applesauce

4 eggs

1 cup unsweetened coconut flakes

1. Preheat the oven to 350 degrees.

2. In the skillet, melt the butter over medium heat. When it's melted, add the carrots. Allow the carrots to simmer in the butter over low to medium heat until the butter is bubbling. Add the pineapple pieces and let them simmer with the carrots on low heat.

3. In a large bowl, combine the cake mix, water, oil, applesauce, eggs, and coconut. Stir to combine.

4. When the butter in the skillet is bubbling, turn off the heat and pour the batter over the carrot/pineapple mix.

5. Bake 35 to 40 minutes until browned on the top and sides and a toothpick inserted in the middle comes out clean.

6. Allow to cool for about 10 minutes. The skillet will still be hot. Put a large serving plate on the counter and, working quickly and deliberately, flip the skillet so the cake is inverted onto the plate.

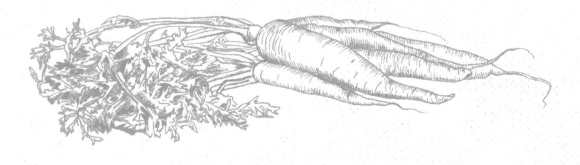

CARAMEL RAISIN SPICE CAKE

SERVES 8 ✦ ACTIVE TIME: 20 MINUTES ✦ START TO FINISH: 60 MINUTES

It's so much fun to shop for add-ins to cake mixes! When I discovered caramel raisins, I couldn't resist adding them to a spice cake mix—along with some chopped nuts. Here's the recipe. See if your family enjoys it as much as mine did (with a scoop of butter pecan ice cream).

8 tablespoons (1 stick) butter

1 (15.25-oz.) box of spice cake mix

1 (8-oz.) package caramel raisins

½ cup chopped walnuts (or almonds or pecans)

1 cup water

½ cup vegetable oil

6 oz. unsweetened applesauce

4 eggs

1. Preheat the oven to 350 degrees.

2. In the skillet, melt the butter over low to medium heat.

3. In a large bowl, combine the cake mix, caramel raisins, nuts, water, oil, applesauce, and eggs. Stir to combine.

4. When the butter in the skillet is melted and hot, pour the batter over it.

5. Bake 30 minutes until browned on the top and sides and a toothpick inserted in the middle comes out clean.

6. Allow to cool for about 10 minutes. The skillet will still be hot. Put a large serving plate on the counter and, working quickly and deliberately, flip the skillet so the cake is inverted onto the plate. Allow to cool an additional 15 to 20 minutes before serving.

FRUIT CUP CAKE

SERVES 8 ✦ ACTIVE TIME: 20 MINUTES ✦ START TO FINISH: 60 MINUTES

Your kids will love this cake—and you will, too! The fruit cup is baked into the cake—with lots of butter—like an upside down cake. Moist and delicious and pretty—a winning combination.

8 tablespoons (1 stick) butter

1 (15-oz.) can no sugar added mixed fruit, drained

1 (15.25-oz.) box of yellow cake mix

1 cup water

½ cup vegetable oil

6 oz. unsweetened applesauce

4 eggs

1. Preheat the oven to 350 degrees.

2. In the skillet, melt the butter over medium heat. When it's melted, add the mixed fruit and distribute evenly in the skillet. Lower the heat but continue to cook.

3. In a large bowl, combine the cake mix, water, oil, applesauce, and eggs. Stir to combine.

4. The fruit-butter mix should be just about bubbling. Pour the batter over it.

5. Bake 35 to 40 minutes until golden brown on the top and sides and a toothpick inserted in the middle comes out clean.

6. Allow to cool for about 10 minutes. The skillet will still be hot. Put a large serving plate on the counter and, working quickly and deliberately, flip the skillet so the cake is inverted onto the plate. Cool to room temperature before serving.

CHOCOLATE CHIP CAKE

SERVES 8 ✦ ACTIVE TIME: 20 MINUTES ✦ START TO FINISH: 60 MINUTES

The result of mixing mini chocolate chips into the cake batter and then cooking it, is that the chips create a very fun polka-dot pattern through the cake. I like to serve this cake with a fruit salad of strawberries, blueberries, cherries, and watermelon pieces.

8 tablespoons (1 stick) butter

1 (15.25-oz.) box of yellow cake mix

1 cup water

½ cup vegetable oil

6 oz. unsweetened applesauce

4 eggs

1 cup mini semi-sweet chocolate morsels

1. Preheat the oven to 350 degrees.

2. In the skillet, melt the butter over low to medium heat.

3. In a large bowl, combine the cake mix, water, oil, applesauce, eggs, and chocolate morsels. Stir to combine.

4. When the butter in the skillet is melted, turn off the heat and pour in the batter.

5. Bake 35 to 40 minutes until golden brown on the top and sides and a toothpick inserted in the middle comes out clean.

6. Allow to cool for about 10 minutes. The skillet will still be hot. Put a large serving plate on the counter and, working quickly and deliberately, flip the skillet so the cake is inverted onto the plate. Cool to room temperature before serving.

ALMOND-CRUSTED RED VELVET CAKE

SERVES 8 ✦ ACTIVE TIME: 20 MINUTES ✦ START TO FINISH: 60 MINUTES

This cake verges on the elegant—there's something about red velvet that looks exotic and special—and can be served with no regrets at a dinner party. The butter-brown sugar-almond topping is crunchy and delicious.

8 tablespoons (1 stick) butter

½ cup dark brown sugar

1 cup sliced almonds

1 (15.25-oz.) box of red velvet cake mix

1 cup water

½ cup vegetable oil

6 oz. unsweetened applesauce

4 eggs

1. Preheat the oven to 350 degrees.

2. In the skillet, melt the butter over medium heat. When thoroughly melted and just starting to bubble, sprinkle the brown sugar over it, then distribute the sliced almonds evenly over the butter/sugar mix. Lower the heat but continue to cook until the butter is just bubbling.

3. In a large bowl, combine the cake mix, water, oil, applesauce, and eggs. Stir to combine.

4. When the butter in the skillet is melted, turn off the heat and pour in the batter.

5. Bake 35 to 40 minutes until golden brown on the top and sides and a toothpick inserted in the middle comes out clean.

6. Allow to cool for about 15 minutes. Run a spatula around the edges and toward the bottom to be sure to loosen any sugar or nuts. Put a large serving plate on the counter and, working quickly and deliberately, flip the skillet so the cake is inverted onto the plate. Cool to room temperature before serving.

COCONUT BROWN SUGAR CAKE

SERVES 8 ✦ ACTIVE TIME: 20 MINUTES ✦ START TO FINISH: 60 MINUTES

It's so great to be able to make cakes that don't need frosting! The butter/sugar mix that the cake cooks in adds all the extra deliciousness that a frosting would. Not only is it fewer calories overall but infinitely easier. Wait until you taste this cake!

8 tablespoons (1 stick) butter

2 tablespoons dark brown sugar

1 (15.25-oz.) box of white cake mix

1 cup unsweetened coconut flakes

½ cup unsweetened shredded coconut

1¼ cups water

⅓ cup vegetable oil

6 oz. unsweetened applesauce

4 eggs

1. Preheat the oven to 350 degrees.

2. In the skillet, melt the butter over medium heat. When it's melted, sprinkle the brown sugar over it. Allow the sugar to melt in the butter over low heat. No need to stir, but don't let the butter get too hot.

3. In a large bowl, combine the cake mix, coconut flakes, shredded coconut, water, oil, applesauce, and eggs. Stir to combine.

4. Pour the batter into the skillet. The butter/sugar mixture will come up over the sides of the batter. It's all part of the magic.

5. Bake 25 to 30 minutes until browned on the top and sides and a toothpick inserted in the middle comes out clean.

6. Allow to cool for about 10 minutes. The skillet will still be hot. Put a large serving plate on the counter and, working quickly and deliberately, flip the skillet so the cake is inverted onto the plate. Allow to cool an additional 15 to 20 minutes before slicing and serving.

7. If you want to dress up this cake, serve with a scoop of vanilla ice cream and a drizzle of raspberry or chocolate sauce.

STRAWBERRY CAKE

SERVES 8 ✦ ACTIVE TIME: 20 MINUTES ✦ START TO FINISH: 60 MINUTES

Pink cake makes you feel happy, that's just a fact. This one won't disappoint. Make it as an every-day cake, or dress it up with a whipped cream frosting and pink sugar for Valentine's Day, Mother's Day, or your daughter's birthday.

1 (14-oz.) bag frozen sliced strawberries, thawed and juice set aside

1 cup strawberry juice and water

8 tablespoons (1 stick) butter

1 (15.25-oz.) box of strawberry or white cake mix

½ cup vegetable oil

6 oz. unsweetened applesauce

4 eggs

1. Preheat the oven to 350 degrees.

2. Set the bag of frozen strawberry pieces in a colander or strainer over a large measuring cup while they thaw so the juices are collected. Transfer thawed berries to a bowl, and add enough water to fill to 1 cup of liquid in the measuring cup.

3. In the skillet, melt the butter over low to medium heat.

4. In a large bowl, combine the strawberry pieces, strawberry water, cake mix, oil, applesauce, and eggs. Stir to combine.

5. Pour the batter over the butter. Bake 35 to 40 minutes until golden brown on the top and sides and a toothpick inserted in the middle comes out clean.

6. Allow to cool for about 10 minutes. The skillet will still be hot. Put a large serving plate on the counter and, working quickly and deliberately, flip the skillet so the cake is inverted onto the plate. Cool to room temperature before serving.

GERMAN CHOCOLATE CAKE

SERVES 8 ✦ ACTIVE TIME: 20 MINUTES ✦ START TO FINISH: 60 MINUTES

By adding some chocolate malt to a devil's food cake mix—and lots of yummy coconut—this cake takes on a distinctive flavor that's rich without being overly sweet. Which means you can put a layer of gooey coconut-pecan frosting on it and really indulge.

8 tablespoons (1 stick) butter

1 (15.25-oz.) box of devil's food cake mix

⅓ cup chocolate Ovaltine

1 cup unsweetened coconut flakes

1 cup water

½ cup vegetable oil

6 oz. unsweetened applesauce

4 eggs

1. Preheat the oven to 350 degrees.

2. In the skillet, melt the butter over low to medium heat.

3. In a large bowl, combine the cake mix, Ovaltine, coconut flakes, water, oil, applesauce, and eggs. Stir to combine.

4. Pour the batter over the butter. Bake 25 to 30 minutes until browned on the top and sides and a toothpick inserted in the middle comes out clean.

5. Allow to cool for about 10 minutes. The skillet will still be hot. Put a large serving plate on the counter and, working quickly and deliberately, flip the skillet so the cake is inverted onto the plate. Allow to cool an additional 15 to 20 minutes before slicing and serving.

COCONUT-PECAN FROSTING

Makes enough to top one layer.

½ cup evaporated milk

½ cup sugar

1 egg yolk

4 tablespoons (¼ cup) butter, cut into slices

½ teaspoon vanilla extract

½ cup sweetened flaked coconut

½ cup chopped pecans

1. In a large saucepan, combine the evaporated milk, sugar, egg yolk, butter, and vanilla. Cook over medium heat, stirring frequently, until thickened, about 10 to 12 minutes. Add the coconut and pecans, stirring to combine. Allow to cool, stirring occasionally. Spread over the top of the cooled skillet cake and refrigerate until ready to serve.

BLACK FOREST CAKE

SERVES 8 • **ACTIVE TIME: 20 MINUTES** • **START TO FINISH: 60 MINUTES**

This is a cake that combines cherries and chocolate—a great pairing! Using canned cherries and cake mix makes preparation simple, but the result is decadently good.

1 (15-oz.) can pitted dark cherries in heavy syrup

1 cup water/syrup combination

8 tablespoons (1 stick) butter

2 tablespoons dark brown sugar

1 (15.25-oz.) box of chocolate fudge cake mix

2 tablespoons unsweetened cocoa powder

½ cup vegetable oil

6 oz. unsweetened applesauce

4 eggs

1. Preheat the oven to 350 degrees.

2. Drain the syrup from the cherries into a measuring cup. Top with water to yield 1 cup of liquid. Chop the cherries into halves or quarters.

3. In the skillet, melt the butter over medium heat. When it's melted, sprinkle the brown sugar over it. Allow the sugar to melt in the butter over low heat. No need to stir, but don't let the butter get too hot.

4. In a large bowl, combine the chopped cherries, syrup/water, cake mix, cocoa powder, oil, applesauce, and eggs. Stir to mix thoroughly.

5. Pour the batter into the skillet. The butter/sugar mixture will come up over the sides of the batter. It's all part of the magic.

6. Bake 25 to 30 minutes until browned on the top and sides and a toothpick inserted in the middle comes out clean.

7. Allow to cool for about 10 minutes. The skillet will still be hot. Put a large serving plate on the counter and, working quickly and deliberately, flip the skillet so the cake is inverted onto the plate. Allow to cool an additional 15 to 20 minutes before slicing and serving.

8. Serve with a scoop of black cherry ice cream. That's it!

PEACHY KEEN CAKE

SERVES 8 ✦ ACTIVE TIME: 20 MINUTES ✦ START TO FINISH: 60 MINUTES

If you find yourself yearning for the taste of juicy peaches and they're not in season, whip up this cake. It'll get you through until the real thing is available. And when you can use ripe peaches instead of canned peaches, just make the switch. The cake will taste equally wonderful. I like to add a touch of almond extract as I think it complements and enhances the peach flavor.

8 tablespoons (1 stick) butter

1 can sliced or chopped peaches with no sugar added, drained

1 (15.25-oz.) box of yellow cake mix

1 cup water

½ cup vegetable oil

6 oz. unsweetened applesauce

4 eggs

¼ teaspoon almond extract

1. Preheat the oven to 350 degrees.

2. In the skillet, melt the butter over medium heat. When it's melted, add the fruit. Allow the fruit to simmer in the butter over low to medium heat until the butter is bubbling but not browning.

3. In a large bowl, combine the cake mix, water, oil, applesauce, eggs, and almond extract. Stir to combine.

4. When the butter in the skillet is bubbling, turn off the heat and pour the batter over the fruit.

5. Bake 35 to 40 minutes until browned on the top and sides and a toothpick inserted in the middle comes out clean.

6. Allow to cool for about 10 minutes. The skillet will still be hot. Put a large serving plate on the counter and, working quickly and deliberately, flip the skillet so the cake is inverted onto the plate. Serve with butter pecan ice cream for a flavor sensation!

SPICY NICEY CAKE

SERVES 8 ✦ ACTIVE TIME: 20 MINUTES ✦ START TO FINISH: 60 MINUTES

I gave this easy-to-make and ready-to-eat cake the funny name because it is a spice cake with a yummy granola/nut crust on top. I also mixed in unsweetened coconut flakes and flax seeds to give more flavor and goodness. So yes, it's a spice cake, but it's so much nicer with the chewy and healthy additions.

8 tablespoons (1 stick) butter

1 cup granola

1 (15.25-oz.) box of spice cake mix

1 cup water

¾ cup vegetable oil

6 oz. unsweetened applesauce

4 eggs

1 cup unsweetened flaked coconut

¼ cup whole flax seeds

1. Preheat the oven to 350 degrees.

2. In the skillet, melt the butter over medium heat. When it's melted, stir in the granola. Allow the granola and butter to cook over low to medium heat until the butter is bubbling but not browning.

3. In a large bowl, combine the cake mix, water, oil, applesauce, eggs, coconut, and flax seeds. Stir to combine.

4. When the butter in the skillet is bubbling, turn off the heat and pour the batter over the granola.

5. Bake 35 to 40 minutes until browned on the top and sides and a toothpick inserted in the middle comes out clean.

6. Allow to cool for about 10 minutes. The skillet will still be hot. Put a large serving plate on the counter and, working quickly and deliberately, flip the skillet so the cake is inverted onto the plate.

7. Enjoy as-is or serve with whipped cream or ice cream.

TROPICAL CAKE

SERVES 8 ✦ ACTIVE TIME: 20 MINUTES ✦ START TO FINISH: 60 MINUTES

Turn up the heat and put on a grass skirt—this cake combines tropical flavors that will transport you to a place south of the Equator. Make this part of a "staycation" luau and serve along with piña coladas, coconut-lime grilled shrimp, rum-glazed spare ribs, avocado and grapefruit salad, and a sense of adventure.

8 tablespoons (1 stick) butter

¾ cup chopped peaches with no sugar added, drained

¾ cup chopped mangos with no sugar added, drained

1 (15.25-oz.) box of yellow cake mix

1 cup unsweetened coconut milk

½ cup vegetable oil

6 oz. unsweetened applesauce

½ cup flaked coconut (sweetened or unsweeted)

4 eggs

1 teaspoon vanilla extract

1. Preheat the oven to 350 degrees.

2. In the skillet, melt the butter over medium heat. When it's melted, add the fruit. Allow the fruit to simmer in the butter over low to medium heat until the butter is bubbling but not browning.

3. In a large bowl, combine the cake mix, coconut milk, oil, applesauce, flaked coconut, eggs, and vanilla extract. Stir to combine.

4. When the butter in the skillet is bubbling, turn off the heat and pour the batter over the fruit.

5. Bake 35 to 40 minutes until browned on the top and sides and a toothpick inserted in the middle comes out clean.

6. Allow to cool for about 10 minutes. The skillet will still be hot. Put a large serving plate on the counter and, working quickly and deliberately, flip the skillet so the cake is inverted onto the plate.

COOKIES & OTHER SWEETS

There's more sweet joy in this chapter if you liked the one about cakes and pies. Why? Because this chapter includes more recipes that simplify and streamline the number of steps between baking and eating. For example, when making cookies with a cast-iron skillet, you put all the dough in right away and cook it, then break it up when it's done. You won't have cookies that stack beautifully, but you'll have wedges of crispy-chewy cookies that are amazingly delicious—and you won't have to work in multiple batches. That's great! There are also recipes for special treats like fruit crisps, clafoutis, bread puddings, and even s'mores here. And brownies. Several kinds of brownies. I saved the best for last!

GIANT CHOCOLATE CHIP COOKIE

Yes, your cast-iron skillet is also a great baking sheet—just smaller, and with sides. So why not cook a giant cookie in it? Here's how.

1 cup (2 sticks) butter, softened

½ cup white sugar

1 cup brown sugar

2 eggs

2 teaspoons vanilla extract

1 teaspoon baking soda

2 teaspoons hot water

½ teaspoon salt

2½ cups flour

2 cups semi-sweet chocolate chips

1. Preheat the oven to 375 degrees. Heat the skillet in the oven while making the batter.

2. In a large bowl, cream together the butter and sugars. Add the eggs one at a time, being sure to combine thoroughly before proceeding. Stir in the vanilla.

3. Dissolve the baking soda in the hot water and add to the batter along with the salt. Stir in the flour and chocolate chips.

4. Remove the skillet from the oven and put the batter in it, smoothing the top with a spatula.

5. Put the skillet in the oven and cook until golden, about 15 minutes.

6. Serve with ice cream.

Variation

If you like nuts in your chocolate chip cookies, you can add them here. Mix in ½ cup walnut or almond pieces when adding the flour and chocolate chips.

GIANT CHOCOLATE COCO-RUM COOKIE

SERVES 6 TO 8 ✦ ACTIVE TIME: 20 MINUTES ✦ START TO FINISH: 45 MINUTES

If you're looking for an over-the-top cookie, try this recipe. There's just a hint of rum, but it infuses the cookie with the essence of the islands.

1 cup flour

1 teaspoon salt

½ teaspoon baking soda

8 tablespoons (1 stick) unsalted butter, softened

½ cup light brown sugar

¼ cup granulated sugar

1 large egg

½ teaspoon vanilla extract

1 teaspoon rum (dark is preferable)

½ cup dark chocolate chips

½ cup grated coconut

1. Preheat the oven to 350 degrees. Heat the skillet in the oven while making the batter.

2. In a bowl, combine the flour, salt, and baking soda, whisking to combine well.

3. In a large bowl, combine the butter and sugars and beat until light and fluffy. Add the egg, vanilla, and rum, stirring or beating to combine. Stir in the flour mixture until all ingredients are combined, then fold in the chocolate chips and coconut.

4. Remove the skillet from the oven and distribute the cookie batter over the surface with a spatula, pressing it gently around the pan. Don't press too hard as the dough will soften as it cooks and spread.

5. Bake for about 15 to 20 minutes, until golden brown on top. Remove from oven and allow to cool about 10 minutes before slicing and removing from skillet.

PEANUT BUTTER COOKIE WEDGES

SERVES 6 TO 8 ✦ ACTIVE TIME: 20 MINUTES ✦ START TO FINISH: 45 MINUTES

This is a recipe that melts in your mouth with the creaminess of the peanut butter. Making thin wedges before baking makes it easier to break away pieces of the cookie when it's cooked. There are all kinds of peanut butters available these days. You can choose creamy or chunky, traditional, or all-natural. I prefer creamy, all-natural peanut butter. The oil has a tendency to separate with this kind of peanut butter, so stir it in the jar before measuring it out.

1½ cups flour

1 teaspoon baking soda

Dash of salt

8 tablespoons (1 stick) butter, softened

½ cup dark brown sugar

½ cup granulated sugar

1 egg

½ teaspoon vanilla extract

½ cup peanut butter

1. Preheat the oven to 350 degrees. Heat the skillet in the oven while making the batter.

2. In a bowl, whisk together the flour, baking soda, and salt.

3. In a large bowl, cream together the butter and sugars until light and creamy. Add the egg and vanilla and mix to combine. Stir in the flour, and when it's incorporated, stir in the peanut butter.

4. Remove the skillet from the oven and spread the cookie batter with a spatula to distribute evenly in the skillet. Use a butter knife to cut lines in the dough to form 8 to 10 wedges.

5. Bake for about 15 to 20 minutes until golden brown and cooked through. Allow to cool for 10 minutes before serving.

Variation

Substitute ½ cup almond butter or cashew butter for the peanut butter, or experiment with a nut butter "blend" of ¼ cup each different nut butters. Experiment with different consistencies of the nut butters, too—try using a chunky peanut butter rather than smooth.

KETTLE CORN COOKIE TREATS

SERVES 6 TO 8 ✦ ACTIVE TIME: 20 MINUTES ✦ START TO FINISH: 45 MINUTES

I was excited to learn about this variation on the classic chocolate chip cookie, so I had to try it. Well, it's a winner! The sweet-salty-crunchy characteristics of the kettle corn are just yummy in a cookie.

2½ cups flour

1 teaspoon baking soda

½ teaspoon salt

1 cup (2 sticks) butter, softened

½ cup white sugar

1 cup brown sugar

2 eggs

½ teaspoon vanilla extract

1½ cups kettle corn

1. Preheat the oven to 375 degrees. Heat the skillet in the oven while making the batter.

2. In a bowl, whisk together the flour, baking soda, and salt.

3. In a large bowl, cream together the butter and sugars until light and creamy. Add the eggs one at a time, being sure to combine thoroughly before proceeding. Stir in the vanilla.

4. Add the flour to the butter mixture, stirring to combine thoroughly. Fold in the kettle corn.

5. Remove the skillet from the oven and put the batter in it, distributing evenly with a spatula.

6. Bake for about 15 to 20 minutes until the top is golden. Remove from the oven and allow to cool about 10 minutes before serving.

GLUTEN-FREE SKILLET MACAROON BITES

SERVES 8 ✦ ACTIVE TIME: 15 MINUTES ✦ START TO FINISH: 45 MINUTES

What I love about this recipe—besides the gooey, sweet, sticky, absolutely delicious result—is the fact that it's a much easier way to make this treat than when you have to scoop the macaroons onto a baking sheet. That is messy and time-consuming. With this version, just pour the confection into the skillet, bake, cool, serve, eat.

1½ cups sugar

4 cups unsweetened coconut flakes

4 egg whites

2 teaspoons vanilla extract

¼ teaspoon salt

1. Preheat the oven to 350 degrees. While oven is preheating, put the skillet in it to warm up.

2. In a large bowl, combine the sugar, coconut, egg whites, vanilla, and salt. Stir to combine well.

3. When the oven is preheated, remove the skillet. Put the batter into the pan and put it back in the oven.

4. Bake for 20 to 30 minutes until browned on top.

5. Allow to cool for about 30 minutes before serving. Slice in wedges and use a pie server to remove from the skillet.

OATMEAL BUTTERSCOTCH COOKIE BARS

SERVES 6 TO 8 ✦ ACTIVE TIME: 20 MINUTES ✦ START TO FINISH: 45 MINUTES

Sure you've heard of oatmeal raisin cookies, but as you can see, I like to experiment with different flavor combinations. And in this case, the slightly savory taste of the butterscotch morsels works really well with the oatmeal base!

1¼ cups flour

2 cups quick cooking oatmeal

1 teaspoon baking soda

½ teaspoon salt

¾ cup (1½ sticks) butter, softened

½ cup dark brown sugar

½ cup granulated sugar

1 egg

½ teaspoon vanilla extract

1½ cups butterscotch morsels

1. Preheat the oven to 350 degrees. Heat the skillet in the oven while making the batter.

2. In a bowl, mix together the flour, oatmeal, baking soda, and salt.

3. In a large bowl, cream together the butter and sugars until light and creamy. Add the egg and vanilla and mix to combine. Stir in the flour, and when it's incorporated, stir in the butterscotch morsels.

4. Remove the skillet from the oven and put the batter in it, distributing evenly with a spatula. Use a butter knife to cut lines in the dough to form 8 to 10 wedges.

5. Bake for about 20 to 25 minutes until golden brown and cooked through. Allow to cool for 10 minutes before serving.

Variation

Substitute toffee chips for the butterscotch chips.

CLASSIC SHORTBREAD COOKIE BARS

SERVES 6 TO 8 ✦ ACTIVE TIME: 25 MINUTES ✦ START TO FINISH: 60 MINUTES

Shortbread cookies are wonderfully simple to prepare and so, so yummy. The butter shines through in each flaky bite. They are the perfect treat for a late afternoon pick-me-up served with coffee, tea, or hot chocolate.

1 cup flour

¼ teaspoon salt

¼ cup sugar

8 tablespoons (1 stick) unsalted butter, chilled

½ teaspoon vanilla extract

1. Preheat the oven to 300 degrees. Heat the skillet in the oven while making the dough.

2. In a large bowl, combine the flour, salt, and sugar, whisking to combine.

3. Cut the butter into slices and add to the flour mixture. The best way to work it into the flour is with your hands. As it starts to come together, add the vanilla extract. Work with it until it resembles coarse meal.

4. Gather the dough into a ball. On a lightly floured surface, roll it out into a circle that's just smaller than the surface of the skillet—about 8 inches in diameter. Slice the round into 8 wedges.

5. Remove the skillet from the oven and place the wedges in it to recreate the circle of dough. Bake for about 45 minutes or until the shortbread is a pale golden color. Remove from the oven and allow to cool for about 10 minutes before transferring the cookies to a plate.

ALMOND SHORTBREAD COOKIE WEDGES

SERVES 6 TO 8 ✦ ACTIVE TIME: 25 MINUTES ✦ START TO FINISH: 60 MINUTES

The addition of almond extract in the recipe gives these light, buttery cookies a wonderful nutty flavor and mouth-watering aroma.

1 cup flour

¼ teaspoon salt

¼ cup sugar

8 tablespoons (1 stick) unsalted butter, chilled

1 teaspoon almond extract

1. Preheat the oven to 300 degrees. Heat the skillet in the oven while making the dough.

2. In a large bowl, combine the flour, salt, and sugar, whisking to combine.

3. Cut the butter into slices and add to the flour mixture. The best way to work it into the flour is with your hands. As it starts to come together, add the almond extract. Work with it until it resembles coarse meal.

4. Gather the dough into a ball. On a lightly floured surface, roll it out into a circle that's just smaller than the surface of the skillet—about 8 inches in diameter. Slice the round into 8 wedges.

5. Remove the skillet from the oven and place the wedges in it to recreate the circle of dough. Bake for about 45 minutes or until the shortbread is a pale golden color. Remove from the oven and allow to cool for about 10 minutes before transferring the cookies to a plate.

COCO-OAT BREAKAWAY COOKIES

MAKES 1 LARGE BREAK-APART COOKIE ✦ ACTIVE TIME: 20 MINUTES ✦ START TO FINISH: 45 MINUTES

If you want a not-too-sweet, chewy cookie as a mid-day snack or to put in your kids' lunches without sending them to school with overly processed and sugared foods, you'll love this recipe. You and the kids can break off pieces to the size that you like, which is fun, too.

1 cup quick cooking oats

½ cup unsweetened shredded or flaked coconut

¾ cup flour

½ teaspoon baking soda

½ teaspoon salt

8 tablespoons (1 stick) butter, softened

½ cup dark brown sugar

¼ cup granulated sugar

½ teaspoon vanilla extract

2 eggs

1. Preheat the oven to 350 degrees. Heat the skillet in the oven while making the batter.

2. In a bowl, mix together the oats, coconut, flour, baking soda, and salt.

3. In a large bowl, cream together the butter and sugars until light and creamy. Add the vanilla and the eggs and stir to combine thoroughly. Add the oat mixture and stir until well blended.

4. Remove the skillet from the oven and put the batter in it, smoothing the top with a spatula.

5. Bake for 20 to 25 minutes until the top is golden brown and the cookie is just firm. Remove from the oven and allow to cool about 10 minutes before transferring to a plate to break apart and serve.

GLUTEN-FREE PEAR-CRANBERRY CRUMBLE

SERVES 4 TO 6 ✦ ACTIVE TIME: 30 MINUTES ✦ START TO FINISH: 60 MINUTES

A dessert that will impress and delight in the fall when cranberries are at their freshest. The almond flour complements the pears beautifully. Delicious!

1 tablespoon butter

4 pears

1 teaspoon ginger

1 cup almond flour

½ cup dark brown sugar

8 tablespoons (1 stick) chilled unsalted butter

½ cup unsweetened coconut flakes

¾ cup fresh cranberries or ½ cup dried cranberries

1. Preheat the oven to 350 degrees.

2. Melt 1 tablespoon butter in the skillet over medium heat.

3. Trim the tops and bottoms from the pears, cut into quarters, remove the cores, and cut each quarter in half. Lay the slices in the skillet on the melted butter. Sprinkle the pear slices with ginger. Remove from the heat.

4. In a bowl, combine the flour and brown sugar. Cut the chilled butter into slices. Using your fingers, blend the butter into the flour and sugar until coarse crumbles form. Add the coconut, stirring to combine thoroughly, then fold in the cranberries.

5. Spread the mixture over the pears. Put the skillet in the oven and bake for 15 to 20 minutes, until the sugar is melted and bubbly. Remove from the oven and let cool for a few minutes before serving. Top with whipped cream or Greek yogurt.

PEAR-GINGER CRUMBLE

SERVES 4 TO 6 ✦ ACTIVE TIME: 30 MINUTES ✦ START TO FINISH: 90 MINUTES

This is a lovely dessert to put together on a fall night, when pears are ripe and the ginger adds a deep warmth to the flavors. Serving it warm is most delicious, but if you can't, no worries—it still tastes great!

1 tablespoon butter

4 pears

1 teaspoon ginger

1 cup flour

½ cup dark brown sugar

8 tablespoons (1 stick) unsalted butter, chilled

½ cup rolled oats

Vanilla ice cream or whipped cream

1. Preheat the oven to 350 degrees.

2. Melt 1 tablespoon butter in the skillet over medium heat.

3. Trim the tops and bottoms from the pears, cut into quarters, remove the cores, and cut each quarter in half. Lay the slices in the skillet on the melted butter. Sprinkle the pear slices with ginger. Remove from the heat.

4. In a bowl, combine the flour and brown sugar. Cut the chilled butter into slices. Using your fingers, blend the butter into the flour and sugar until coarse crumbles form. Add the rolled oats. Spread the mixture over the pears. Put the skillet in the oven and bake for 15 minutes, until the sugar is melted and bubbly. Remove from the oven and let cool for a few minutes before serving. Top with ice cream or whipped cream.

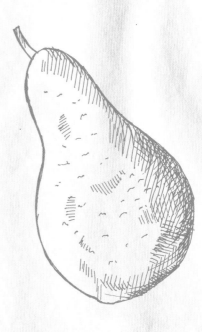

APPLE-PEAR CRISP

SERVES 6 TO 8 ✦ ACTIVE TIME: 40 MINUTES ✦ START TO FINISH: 60 MINUTES

The flavors of fall shine in this dish, which is a winner every time.

Topping

½ cup walnut pieces, preferably toasted

3 tablespoons light brown sugar

2 tablespoons butter, softened

½ teaspoon cinnamon

¼ teaspoon freshly grated nutmeg

¼ teaspoon salt

Apples & Pears

1 tablespoon butter

1 apple, peeled, cored, and sliced

1 pear, cored and sliced

1 teaspoon fresh lemon juice

1 teaspoon maple syrup

Butter pecan ice cream

1. Preheat the oven to 350 degrees.

2. In a small bowl, combine the nuts, sugar, butter, cinnamon, nutmeg, and salt. Using your fingers, crumble it up until it's somewhat combined. No need to get too particular about it.

3. Heat the butter in a skillet over medium-high heat. Add the apple slices and cook, stirring gently, for a minute or so, then add the pear slices and continue to cook until the fruits soften. Sprinkle the lemon juice and maple syrup over the fruits and remove from heat.

4. Using your fingers, spread the nut/sugar mixture over the top of the fruits. Put the skillet in the oven and cook for about 10 minutes, until the fruits are bubbling and the topping is lightly toasted. Serve with butter pecan ice cream for a true taste treat.

Variations

✸ Instead of walnuts, use pecan pieces or crushed almonds.

✸ Cut the amount of nuts by half and use oatmeal for the additional amount.

✸ Instead of an apple-pear combo, make it with just one of these fruits, doubling up on the one you select. Add a handful of dried cranberries while the fruits are sautéing.

STRAWBERRY RHUBARB CRISP

SERVES 4 ✦ ACTIVE TIME: 30 MINUTES ✦ START TO FINISH: 60 MINUTES

Nothing says early summer like fresh, juicy strawberries. Rhubarb contributes texture and tartness to cooked strawberries. Together, they're magic.

1½ cups rhubarb, cut into ½-inch pieces

1½ cups strawberries, sliced

2 tablespoons sugar

2 teaspoons flour

4 tablespoons butter, chilled, cut into pieces

¼ cup dark brown sugar

¾ cup oats (quick cooking but not instant)

⅓ cup flour

1. Preheat the oven to 450 degrees.

2. In a bowl, combine the rhubarb pieces, strawberry slices, sugar, and flour, and toss to coat the fruit. Transfer to the skillet.

3. In another bowl, work the butter in with the sugar using a fork. Add the oats and flour and continue to work with the fork to create a crumbly mix. Sprinkle it over the fruit in the skillet.

4. Put the skillet in the oven and bake for about 30 minutes until the topping is golden and the fruit is bubbly. Serve warm with whipped cream or ice cream.

In the early 1900s, American rhubarb farmers successfully lobbied for their vegetable to be officially designated as a fruit so that they could get lower tax rates and less stringent interstate shipping laws.

PEACH CRISP

SERVES 4 TO 6 ✦ ACTIVE TIME: 30 MINUTES ✦ START TO FINISH: 60 MINUTES

Just like a strawberry-rhubarb crisp says early summer, so a fresh peach crisp says late summer. Use ripe fruit and plenty of it and you may want to make this every night while peaches are in season.

5 or 6 peaches, pitted and sliced (skin on or off)

¼ cup sugar to mix with the peaches

1 to 2 tablespoons flour

¾ cup flour

¼ teaspoon salt

½ cup sugar for the topping

¼ cup dark brown sugar

8 tablespoons (1 stick) chilled butter, cut into pieces

½ cup oats (quick-cooking but not instant)

1. Preheat the oven to 350 degrees.

2. In a bowl, combine peach slices with sugar and flour. The amount of flour you use will depend on how juicy the peaches are—more juice means more flour. Let the peaches sit in the bowl while you make the topping. If there's juice in the bowl after sitting, add another tablespoon of flour.

3. In another bowl, make the topping. Blend the flour, salt, and both sugars together, and add the butter, using a fork to combine them. When somewhat mixed and crumbly, add the oats and stir. The topping should be crumbly.

4. Put the peaches in the skillet and top with the crumbly dough.

5. Put in the oven and bake for about 1 hour until the topping is golden and the peaches are bubbling. If it doesn't look crispy enough, turn the oven up to 375 degrees and continue to bake, checking every 5 minutes until it looks just right. Be careful not to burn the topping.

6. Serve warm with fresh whipped cream and a sprinkling of toasted nuts.

Variation

Many fruit crisp recipes feature nuts in the topping. These can be whatever you like: walnuts, pecans, or almonds. Break the raw nuts into pieces and use about ½ cup in the topping.

BAKED APPLES

SERVES 4 ✦ ACTIVE TIME: 30 MINUTES ✦ START TO FINISH: 50 MINUTES

These are easy to make and are delicious served warm or at room temperature the next day. Of course, they're best with a side of vanilla ice cream or even maple Greek yogurt.

4 firm apples

2 tablespoons butter

½ cup water

Maple syrup

1. Preheat the oven to 350 degrees.

2. Peel the apples, leaving a ring of peel on the bottom where the apple will stand in the skillet. Get as much of the core out without cutting the apple in half.

3. Heat the skillet over medium-high. Add the butter and let it melt. Place the apples bottom-down in the skillet. Add the water from the center so that it distributes evenly around the apples. Drizzle the tops of the apples with maple syrup.

4. Put the skillet in the oven and cook for about 20 minutes, or until apples are soft. Drizzle with additional maple syrup if desired.

Variations

✹ Use apple cider instead of water to make a nice apple-butter sauce, which you can simmer down after the apples are cooked to make a concentrated sauce.

✹ Paleo-friendy Variation: This recipe is easily Paleo-appropriate with the substitution of 2 tablespoons coconut oil or ghee (clarified butter) for the butter.

DUTCH APPLE BABY

SERVES 4 ✦ ACTIVE TIME: 45 MINUTES ✦ START TO FINISH: 75 MINUTES

This is a classic cast-iron skillet recipe for a pastry that puffs in the oven. It is reminiscent of the recipe for Eyre's pancakes in the Breakfast chapter.

2 firm, semi-tart apples, like Mutsu or Golden Delicious

4 tablespoons butter

¼ cup sugar

1 tablespoon cinnamon

3 tablespoons sugar

¾ cup flour

¼ teaspoon salt

¾ cup milk

4 eggs

1 teaspoon vanilla or almond extract

Confectioner's sugar for dusting

1. Preheat the oven to 425 degrees and position a rack in the middle.

2. Peel and core the apples, and cut into slices. Heat a skillet over medium-high heat. Add the butter and apples and cook, stirring, for 3 to 4 minutes until the apples soften. Add the sugar and cinnamon and continue cooking for another 3 or 4 minutes. Distribute the apples evenly over the bottom of the skillet and remove from heat.

3. In a large bowl, mix the flour and salt. In a smaller bowl, whisk together the milk, eggs, and vanilla or almond extract. Add the wet ingredients to the dry ingredients and stir to combine. Pour the batter over the apples.

4. Put the skillet in the oven and bake for 15 to 20 minutes until the "baby" is puffed and browned on the top.

5. Remove from the oven and allow to cool for a few minutes. Run a knife along the edge of the skillet to loosen the dessert. Put a plate over the skillet and, using oven mitts or pot holders, flip the skillet over so the dessert is transferred to the plate. Serve warm with a dusting of confectioner's sugar.

The Dutch Apple Baby is attributed to early Pennsylvania Dutch settlers.

SKILLET S'MORES

SERVES 6 TO 8 ✦ ACTIVE TIME: 20 MINUTES ✦ START TO FINISH: 30 MINUTES

If you planned a cookout and the weather didn't cooperate, trust your cast-iron skillet to save the evening when you gather the kids and others around to share this campfire treat.

1 (16.5-oz.) bag semi-sweet chocolate chips

16 marshmallows, cut in half

Graham crackers

1. Preheat the oven to 450 degrees.

2. Put the chocolate chips in the skillet and top with the cut marshmallows, clean side facing up.

3. Bake in the oven until marshmallows brown on top, about 5 minutes.

4. Serve with graham crackers for scooping and a side of ghost stories.

Americans eat more marshmallows than any other country, maybe because the modern manufacturing of them was established in the Chicago area in the early 1950s by Duomak. The confection we enjoy today is far removed from its original source—the root of the Althaea officinalis, a marshland flower. It was the ancient Egyptians who first extracted its sweet sap.

Today's commercially available marshmallows are made with spun sugar, water, and gelatin. More and more confectionery retailers are offering homemade marshmallows, and it's not difficult to make them yourself. They are yummy!

CHERRY CLAFOUTI

SERVES 4 TO 6 ✦ ACTIVE TIME: 20 MINUTES ✦ START TO FINISH: 45 MINUTES

Another French specialty that originated in the Limousin region and used the sour cherries that grew there, the dessert is so delicious that it is now known around the world. It's essentially full-flavored cherries baked in a custard. How can you go wrong?

8 tablespoons (1 stick) butter, melted

½ cup sugar

⅔ cup flour

½ teaspoon salt

1 teaspoon vanilla extract

3 eggs, beaten

1 cup milk

2 tablespoons unsalted butter

3 cups ripe cherries (pits in)

½ cup + 2 teaspoons sugar

1. Preheat the oven to 400 degrees.

2. In a large bowl, mix together 6 tablespoons of the butter, sugar, flour, salt, vanilla, eggs, and milk until all ingredients are blended and smooth. Set aside.

3. Put 2 tablespoons of butter in the skillet and put it in the oven to heat up.

4. Transfer the skillet to the stovetop and add the additional butter. When it is melted, put the sugar in the skillet and shake it so it distributes evenly. Add the cherries. Pour the batter over the cherries, sprinkle with the last teaspoons of sugar, and put the skillet back in the oven. Bake for about 30 minutes, or until the topping is golden brown and set in the center.

5. Serve warm—and be sure to let diners know that the cherries contain their pits.

The Limousin region of France is located in the center of the country, with Bordeaux to the west and Lyon to the east. Limoges is the largest city in the region. It is known for its agricultural heritage, including the griottes (sour morello cherries) grown there. There is some debate about whether the pits should be removed from the cherries before baking, but even Julia Child left them in, going with the belief that the pits add flavor.

PEAR CLAFOUTI

SERVES 4 TO 6 ✦ ACTIVE TIME: 20 MINUTES ✦ START TO FINISH: 45 MINUTES

When you get the hang of making clafouti, you'll want to experiment making it with different fruits. This one is made with pears and instead of vanilla extract has almond extract to accentuate their mild nuttiness.

8 tablespoons (1 stick) melted butter

½ cup sugar

⅔ cup flour

½ teaspoon salt

1 teaspoon almond extract

3 eggs

1 cup milk

4 tablespoons unsalted butter

4 pears

½ cup + 2 teaspoons sugar

1. Preheat the oven to 400 degrees.

2. In a large bowl, mix together 6 tablespoons of the butter, sugar, flour, salt, almond extract, eggs, and milk until all ingredients are blended and smooth. Set aside.

3. Put 2 tablespoons of butter in the skillet and put it in the oven to heat up.

4. In another skillet on the stove, working over medium-high heat, add the additional butter until melted. Add the fruit and sugar to the butter and cook, stirring, until the pears are just soft and glazed, about 3 minutes.

5. Remove the skillet from the oven and pour in half the batter. Spoon the cooked pears over the batter, and then add the remaining batter. Sprinkle with the sugar.

6. Bake in the oven for 25 to 30 minutes until the clafouti is golden brown and set in the center. Serve warm with whipped cream or confectioner's sugar if desired, or just by itself.

Although clafouti is most delicious served warm, it is plenty tasty served at room temperature or even chilled.

CHOCOLATE CRANBERRY BAKE

SERVES 10 TO 12 ✦ ACTIVE TIME: 15 MINUTES ✦ START TO FINISH: 45 MINUTES

This dense, chewy "cake" is great to have with coffee or tea in the afternoon to help boost your energy. The dark chocolate and semi-tart cranberries are a beautiful pairing, and the nuts add extra texture and layers of flavor. Delicious!

5 oz. dried cranberries

¼ cup chopped walnuts

¼ cup chopped almonds

⅓ cup dark chocolate chips

1 cup flour

½ cup sugar

2 eggs

¾ cup butter, melted

1. Preheat the oven to 350 degrees.

2. With the skillet over low heat, spread the cranberries on the bottom. Sprinkle on the walnuts, almonds, and chocolate chips. Let the fruit, chocolate, and nuts stay on low while the batter is prepared.

3. In a bowl, combine the flour, sugar, eggs, and melted butter and mix to combine thoroughly.

4. Spread the dough over the cranberry mixture carefully so it sits on top.

5. Bake for 25 minutes until just golden brown on top. Remove from oven and allow to cool for 10 minutes before inverting onto a larger plate.

BREAD PUDDING

SERVES 8 TO 10 ✦ **ACTIVE TIME: 60 MINUTES** ✦ **START TO FINISH: 2 HOURS**

Whoever invented bread pudding was on to something—use up some slightly stale bread, drench it in butter, sugar, and eggs, and bake. It's a bit trickier than that, but not much. Enjoy!

6 tablespoons butter

1 large baguette, cubed preferably a day old

¼ cup raisins (optional)

⅔ cup toasted almonds or walnuts (optional)

1 cup apples or pears, cored and diced

3 eggs

1½ cups milk

1½ cups heavy cream

1 cup sugar

1 tablespoon vanilla extract

¼ teaspoon cinnamon

⅛ teaspoon nutmeg

⅛ teaspoon ginger

1. Prepare the skillet by coating it with 2 tablespoons of the butter. Make a layer of bread cubes using half the baguette. Sprinkle half of the raisins, nuts, and fruit over the cubes, and make another layer, starting with the bread cubes and topping with the raisins, nuts, and fruit.

2. In a large bowl, whisk the eggs until frothy and add the milk, cream, sugar, vanilla, and spices. Whisk briskly to blend thoroughly. Pour the mixture over the bread layers, shaking the pan slightly to be sure to distribute throughout and so that the top cubes are just moistened while the bottom layer gets most of the liquid.

3. Refrigerate for about an hour, pressing down on the bread occasionally.

4. Preheat the oven to 325 degrees and position a rack in the center. Before putting the skillet in the oven, cut up the remaining 4 tablespoons of butter into little pieces and place them over the top of the pudding. Bake in the oven for 1 hour.

5. Remove and allow to cool for about a half hour. Serve with fresh whipped cream, ice cream, or a Grand Marnier sauce (see below).

GRAND MARNIER SAUCE

6 tablespoons butter

½ cup sugar

½ cup Grand Marnier

1 egg

1. Melt the butter in a heavy-bottomed saucepan over medium heat. Add the sugar and stir constantly with a wooden spoon while it dissolves and begins to cook. Stir until dissolved, about 2 minutes, then stir in the Grand Marnier, continue to cook for a minute or two, and remove from the heat.

2. In a bowl, whisk the egg until frothy. Add a large spoonful of the warm Grand Marnier/sugar sauce to the egg and continue to whisk so that it combines. Transfer this to the saucepan and whisk it in with the rest of the sauce.

3. On low heat, cook the sauce, whisking constantly, until it starts to thicken (about 3 minutes). Remove from the heat and continue to whisk as it thickens. Drizzle it over bread pudding, or serve on the side.

BUTTER PECAN BREAD PUDDING

SERVES 4 TO 6 ✦ ACTIVE TIME: 45 MINUTES ✦ START TO FINISH: 2 HOURS

If you want a super-simple, irresistible recipe for no-fail bread pudding, look no further. The addition of toasted pecan pieces sets this dish apart. The better the quality of the ice cream, the tastier the bread pudding will be and the better it will set up.

½ cup chopped pecans

4 tablespoons butter

4 cups cubed bread from a day-old loaf of French or Italian bread

2 eggs

¼ cup rum

1 gallon vanilla ice cream, left out to soften (high-quality so that it is as rich as possible)

1. Place the skillet over medium-high heat. When hot, add the chopped pecans. Using pot holders or oven mitts, shake the pecans in the skillet while they cook. You want them to toast but not brown or burn. This should take just a few minutes.

2. When toasted, transfer the pecans to a plate and allow to cool.

3. Add the butter to the skillet and, over low heat, let it melt. Add the bread pieces to the skillet and distribute evenly. Sprinkle the pecan pieces over the bread cubes.

4. In a bowl, whisk the eggs with the rum. Add the softened or melted ice cream and stir just enough to combine. Pour the egg/ice cream mixture over the bread and nuts. Shake the skillet gently to distribute the liquid evenly.

5. Cover with plastic wrap, put in a cool place, and allow the mixture to rest for about 30 minutes so that the bread cubes are saturated with the ice cream.

6. Preheat the oven to 350 degrees.

7. Bake for 40 to 45 minutes until the cream mixture is set and it is slightly brown around the edges. Use pot holders or oven mitts to take the skillet out of the oven. Allow to cool for 5 to 10 minutes before inverting onto a serving dish. Serve immediately. No need for additional ice cream.

KILLER VANILLA BREAD PUDDING

SERVES 4 TO 6 ✦ ACTIVE TIME: 45 MINUTES ✦ START TO FINISH: 2 HOURS

Here's another variation on delicious and easy bread pudding that is sure to be loved by all members of the family. This is an easy, last-minute dessert you can throw together that will be gobbled up when it comes out of the oven—guaranteed! An important note, though: use high-quality ice cream so that it is as rich as possible.

4 tablespoons butter

4 cups cubed pieces of croissants or a combination of baguette and croissant

2 eggs

1 teaspoon vanilla extract

1 gallon vanilla ice cream, left out to soften (high-quality so that it is as rich as possible)

1. Place the skillet over low heat. Melt the butter in the skillet. Add the bread pieces to the skillet and distribute evenly.

2. In a bowl, whisk the eggs and vanilla. Add the softened or melted ice cream and stir just enough to combine. Pour the egg/ice cream mixture over the bread. Shake the skillet gently to distribute the liquid evenly.

3. Cover with plastic wrap, put in a cool place, and allow the mixture to rest for about 30 minutes so that the bread cubes are saturated with the ice cream.

4. Preheat the oven to 350 degrees.

5. Bake for 40 to 45 minutes until the cream mixture is set and it is slightly brown around the edges. Use pot holders or oven mitts to take the skillet out of the oven. Allow to cool for 5 to 10 minutes before inverting onto a serving dish. Serve immediately. No need for additional ice cream.

RED, WHITE, AND BLUE BREAD PUDDING

SERVES 4 TO 6 ✦ ACTIVE TIME: 45 MINUTES ✦ START TO FINISH: 2 HOURS

This is one to make around 4th of July—or almost any time in the summer, as it just pops with the flavors of these fruits.

4 tablespoons butter

4 cups cubed bread from a day-old loaf of French or Italian bread

1 cup fresh or frozen blueberries

2 eggs

1 gallon strawberry ice cream, left out to soften (high-quality so that it is as rich as possible)

1. Place the skillet over low heat. Melt the butter in the skillet. Add the bread pieces to the skillet and distribute evenly. Sprinkle the blueberries over the bread pieces.

2. In a bowl, whisk the eggs. Add the softened or melted ice cream and stir just enough to combine. Pour the egg/ice cream mixture over the bread. Shake the skillet gently to distribute the liquid evenly.

3. Cover with plastic wrap, put in a cool place, and allow the mixture to rest for about 30 minutes so that the bread cubes are saturated with the ice cream.

4. Preheat the oven to 350 degrees.

5. Bake for 40 to 45 minutes until the cream mixture is set and it is slightly brown around the edges. Use pot holders or oven mitts to take the skillet out of the oven. Allow to cool for 5 to 10 minutes before inverting onto a serving dish. Serve immediately. No need for additional ice cream.

BEER BROWNIES

SERVES 6 TO 8 ✦ ACTIVE TIME: 30 MINUTES ✦ START TO FINISH: 90 MINUTES

Here's something different and fun that will make you the hit of the party. Stout is a dark beer traditionally made with roasted malt or barley, plus hops, water, and yeast. Choose a chocolate or coffee stout to really complement the chocolate and espresso that are also in the recipe. The beer gives an extra depth and earthiness to the gooey chocolate deliciousness of this brownie. Serve with—what else?—chocolate stout!

8 tablespoons (1 stick) unsalted butter

½ cup dark chocolate morsels or 4 oz. 60% dark chocolate broken into pieces

½ cup stout (chocolate or coffee)

2 eggs

⅔ cup sugar

½ cup flour

2 tablespoons unsweetened cocoa powder

1 tablespoon espresso powder

¼ teaspoon salt

1. Preheat the oven to 350 degrees.

2. Melt the butter in the skillet over medium heat. Add the chocolate pieces and stir until melted. Add the beer, stir to combine, and remove from the heat.

3. In a bowl, whisk together the eggs and sugar until combined. In a separate bowl, stir together the flour, cocoa powder, espresso powder, and salt. Add to the egg/sugar mix, whisking until just combined. Pour this batter over the chocolate in the skillet and stir gently until just combined.

4. Bake for 25 to 30 minutes, until the top has set and a toothpick inserted in the middle comes out with just some crumbs. Be careful not to overbake.

5. Remove from the oven and allow to cool 10 to 15 minutes before serving.

THE BEST SKILLET BROWNIES

SERVES 6 TO 8 ✦ ACTIVE TIME: 40 MINUTES ✦ START TO FINISH: 90 MINUTES

If you're serious about chocolate brownies, you'll love this recipe. When shopping for the ingredients, remember that the better quality the chocolate, the better the taste and texture of the brownie. What is baked up in the cast-iron skillet is a gooey yet crunchy confection that is heaven in every bite. Don't even wait to slice and serve it—eat it right out of the skillet (when it's cool enough). Be sure to have friends and family around when you do, as you may be tempted to eat the whole thing by yourself, and that wouldn't be good.

10 tablespoons unsalted butter

8 oz. semi-sweet chocolate, coarsely chopped

1 cup sugar

3 eggs at room temperature

1 teaspoon vanilla extract

½ cup + 2 tablespoons all-purpose flour

2 tablespoons unsweetened cocoa powder

¼ teaspoon salt

1 cup semi-sweet chocolate chips

1. Preheat the oven to 350 degrees.

2. In a microwave-safe bowl, melt the butter and chocolate pieces together, cooking in 15-second increments and stirring after each increment. The butter and chocolate should be just melted together and smooth.

3. In a large bowl, whisk the sugar in with the eggs. Add the vanilla and stir to combine. Working in batches, start mixing the melted chocolate into the sugar/egg mixture, stirring vigorously to combine after each addition. In a small bowl, mix the flour, cocoa powder, and salt. Gently fold the dry ingredients into the chocolate mix. Next, fold in the chocolate chips.

4. Over medium heat, melt 1 tablespoon butter in the skillet. When melted, pour in the batter. Bake for about 30 minutes or until a toothpick inserted in the center comes out with a few moist crumbs. It may need a couple more minutes, but be careful not to overbake this or you'll lose the great gooiness. When it's ready, remove from the oven and allow to cool about 10 minutes.

5. Dig right in, or scoop into bowls and serve with your favorite ice cream.

PEPPERMINT DARK CHOCOLATE BROWNIES

SERVES 6 TO 8 ✦ ACTIVE TIME: 40 MINUTES ✦ START TO FINISH: 90 MINUTES

These dark chocolate brownies will blow you away with a blast of fresh peppermint in every bite. You can go as dark as you like with the chocolate, but I think 70% is best.

8 tablespoons (1 stick) unsalted butter + 1 tablespoon

8 oz. dark chocolate, coarsely chopped

1 cup sugar

3 eggs at room temperature

½ teaspoon peppermint extract

½ cup + 2 tablespoons all-purpose flour

2 tablespoons unsweetened cocoa powder

¼ teaspoon salt

1½ cups York Peppermint Patty pieces

1. Preheat the oven to 350 degrees.

2. In a microwave-safe bowl, melt the butter and chocolate pieces together, cooking in 15-second increments and stirring after each increment. The butter and chocolate should be just melted together and smooth.

3. In a large bowl, whisk the sugar in with the eggs. Add the peppermint and stir to combine. Working in batches, start mixing the melted chocolate into the sugar/egg mixture, stirring vigorously to combine after each addition. In a small bowl, mix the flour, cocoa powder, and salt. Gently fold the dry ingredients into the chocolate mix. Next, fold in the Peppermint Patty pieces.

4. Over medium heat, melt 1 tablespoon butter in the skillet. When melted, pour in the batter. Bake for about 30 minutes or until a toothpick inserted in the center comes out with a few moist crumbs. It may need a couple more minutes, but be careful not to overbake this or you'll lose the great gooiness. When it's ready, remove from the oven and allow to cool about 10 minutes. Serve in wedges with mint chocolate chip ice cream.

CHOCOLATE CHEESECAKE BROWNIES

SERVES 6 TO 8 ✦ ACTIVE TIME: 40 MINUTES ✦ START TO FINISH: 90 MINUTES

For this brownie, a swirl of cheesecake batter adds an extra creamy goodness.

8 tablespoons
(1 stick) butter

¼ cup unsweetened
cocoa powder

1 cup sugar

½ cup flour

½ teaspoon salt

2 large eggs, lightly
beaten

1 teaspoon vanilla
extract

1 cup semi-sweet
chocolate chips

Cream Cheese Batter

4 oz. cream cheese,
softened

¼ cup sugar

1 egg

1 teaspoon vanilla
extract

1. Preheat the oven to 325 degrees.

2. Prepare the cream cheese batter by combining the cream cheese, sugar, egg, and vanilla in a bowl. Set aside.

3. Melt butter in the skillet over medium-low heat.

4. Put the cocoa powder in a medium-sized bowl. When the butter is melted, pour it over the cocoa powder, leaving a film of butter on the skillet. Whisk the butter into the chocolate, then add the sugar, stirring to combine. Combine the flour and salt, and stir this into the batter. Add the eggs, vanilla, and chocolate chips and stir to blend.

5. Put the batter into the skillet. Drop the cream cheese batter in spoonfuls onto the brownie, distributing evenly. Use a small knife to gently swirl the cream cheese into the chocolate.

6. Put the skillet in the oven and bake for 30 to 35 minutes until the edges start to brown and a toothpick inserted in the middle comes out clean. Use pot holders or oven mitts to remove the hot skillet. Let it cool for about 10 minutes.

Serve with fresh strawberries or raspberries.

CHOCOLATE ALMOND BROWNIE BITES

MAKES ABOUT 30 PIECES ✦ ACTIVE TIME: 40 MINUTES ✦ START TO FINISH: 90 MINUTES

Once you've inverted the skillet brownie onto a platter, you'll want to cut the confection into small bite-sized pieces as this makes a rich, gooey, and decadent dessert or snack.

8 tablespoons (1 stick) butter

¼ cup unsweetened cocoa powder

1 cup sugar

½ teaspoon salt

2 large eggs

1 teaspoon vanilla extract

1 cup semi-sweet chocolate chips

3 teaspoons salted almond butter

1. Preheat the oven to 325 degrees.

2. Melt butter in the skillet over medium-low heat.

3. Put the cocoa powder in a medium-sized bowl. When the butter is melted, pour it over the cocoa powder, leaving a film of butter on the skillet. Whisk the butter into the chocolate, then add the sugar and salt, stirring to combine. Add the eggs one at a time until mixed in, but don't overdo it. Add the vanilla and chocolate chips and stir to blend.

4. Put the batter into the skillet and use a spatula to spread it out. Spoon the almond butter onto a small plate and microwave it for 20 to 30 seconds until it's soft and more spreadable. Drop it in spoonfuls onto the brownie, distributing evenly. Use a small knife to gently swirl the almond butter into the chocolate.

5. Put the skillet in the oven and bake for 35 to 40 minutes until the edges start to brown. Use pot holders or oven mitts to remove the hot skillet. Let it cool for about 10 minutes. Run a spatula around the sides to be sure the brownie is loose, then very carefully invert it onto a large plate. Allow to cool another 5 or more minutes.

6. Cut into bite-sized pieces and store in an airtight container, layering the bites between waxed paper. Keep in a cool place or refrigerate.

ABOUT CIDER MILL PRESS BOOK PUBLISHERS

Good ideas ripen with time. From seed to harvest, Cider Mill Press brings fine reading, information, and entertainment together between the covers of its creatively crafted books. Our Cider Mill bears fruit twice a year, publishing a new crop of titles each spring and fall.

"Where Good Books Are Ready for Press"

Visit us on the Web at
www.cidermillpress.com
or write to us at
PO Box 454
Kennebunkport, Maine 04046